PRAYERS THAT GET RESULTS

"The DOERS Guide to Turning Tragedy into Triumph and Overcoming the Failures in Life!"

Volume 1

Dr. Kisia L. Coleman

Prayers That Get Results –The DOERS Guide to Turning Tragedy into Triumph and Overcoming the Failures in Life!
By Dr. Kisia L. Coleman
Published by KishKnows, Inc.

Updated Cover Edition

Cover design, editing, book layout and publishing by KishKnows, Inc., Richton Park, Illinois
708-252-DOIT
admin@kishknows.com
www.kishknows.com

ISBN 978-0-9700561-7-7
LCCN 2016908931

All rights reserved. No part of this book may be reproduced or transmitted in any form or by any means, electronic or mechanical, including photocopying and recording, or by any information storage and retrieval system, without permission from the publisher.

Some scripture references are either paraphrased versions or illustrative references of the author. Unless otherwise specified, all other references are King James Versions of the bible.

Copyright © 2016 by Kisia L. Coleman

Printed in the United States of America

DEDICATION

In Memory of

Ada "Madea" Fells

Reginald Coleman

Charnell Coleman

Cynthia Heath-Baldwin

&

Dedicated To

Elder Lillian "Momma" Robinson

and

The 5 Am Prayer Line Prayer Warriors

TABLE OF CONTENTS

INTRODUCTION 1
PRELUDE 5
OPENING PRAYER ACTIVATION 11

SECTION ONE - THE GUIDE: Discovering the DOERS Mindset to Get Results

CHAPTER ONE: Positioning for Prayer 15
CHAPTER TWO: Passionately Pursuing Your Promise 23
CHAPTER THREE: Potency & Power 33
CHAPTER FOUR: Perseverance & Persistence 41
CHAPTER FIVE: Performing the Principles 49
CHAPTER SIX: The Prescription for Your Pain 59

SECTION TWO – THE GAME: Developing the DOERS Strategies for Effective Prayer Initiatives

CHAPTER SEVEN: Hot Stones 69
CHAPTER EIGHT: Rizpah's Rock 73
CHAPTER NINE: Until Heavy Rain Falls 83
CHAPTER TEN: Failure Is Only Feedback 91
CHAPTER ELEVEN: Turning Tragedy into Triumph 97

SECTION THREE – THE GO: Doing It! Going from Information & Impartation to Application & Activation

CHAPTER TWELVE: Prayers that Get Results 111
    Kingly Authority Activation 111
    Priestly Position Activation 113
    Prayers for Children 114
    Prayers Against Premature Death 119
    Prayers for Endurance 121
    Prayer Against Evil 124
    Prayers Against Injustice 125
    Prayers Against Negative Influences 129
    Prayers for Refuge & Shelter 134
    Prayers for Righteous Living 135
    Prayers for God to Be Your Rock 140
    Prayers for Strength 142
    Prayers to Overcome Suffering 144
    Prayers for Vindication 146
ACKNOWLEDGMENTS 151
ADDITIONAL PRAYER RESOURCES ....…..155
AUTHOR BIOGRAPHICAL INFORMATION 156
AUTHOR CONTACT INFORMATION 159

INTRODUCTION

I wrote this book as a response to the cry of my heart to see more supernatural, manifested results of prayer from believers. For years, I have witnessed many intercessors, prayer warriors and even those who consider themselves to be generals, labor in prayer but not receive the fullness of the manifestation that heaven had available for their situation. I believe that there are levels, dimensions and realms in prayer which require certain principles to be practiced and different strategies implemented in order for breakthrough. You can do the right thing the wrong way. Likewise, prayer is the right thing to do but there are certain situations in life that need to be addressed a certain way.

The bible clearly states that it is the effectual, fervent prayer of the righteous person that avails much. If there is an effective, fervent prayer, could it be said that there is an ineffective, dull prayer? Are there prayers being prayed that aren't availing much or at all? You can also make the mistake of praying amiss, which simply means you are praying outside of the will of God. When you pray outside of His will which is His Word, you are asking God to go against Himself. This is something that He is incapable of doing. Therefore, we must align ourselves with the proper information to get results.

Additionally, I believe that the body of Christ in general needs to ascend higher in prayer in the spirit realm. I submit to you that if you are praying the same prayers on the same level from the same dimension that you prayed last year, last month, last week or even yesterday then you might not be as effective as you think. There are shifts taking place in the spirit realm all of the time. We need to make the necessary shifts in our prayer lives to combat the new tactics of the enemy. We should be ascending from glory to glory (2 Corinthians 3:18) and receiving revelation from faith to faith (Romans 1:17) taking us higher and higher in our prayer lives.

You will notice that this is Volume 1, as it is the first of more books along the line of this theme. The book is broken up into three sections. Section 1, 'The Guide' is for the purpose of creating the correct paradigm needed for effective prayer. Section 2, 'The Game' is for the purpose of unfolding how tragic situations occur in life and how you can beat the enemy at his game of trying to stop you. Section 3, 'The Go' is for the purpose of putting into play the information you have received and applying the strategies gained. By the end of this book, you should not only be equipped, but activated to pray prayers that get results and triumph over tragedy.

As one who operates as an intercessor, this is my heart's desire; to graduate and excel in the area of

INTRODUCTION

intercession, manifesting prayer results and assisting the advancement of the Kingdom of Heaven in the earth realm. I am ready to go higher! Will you go with me?

PRELUDE
When Unexpected Tragedy Happens

It was late during the evening of March 14, 2009 when my husband, John and I received what would prove to be the worst phone call of our lives. On the other line was a Chicago Police Department officer that started his communication with words we will never forget, "Is this the brother of Reginald Coleman? Yes, Mr. Coleman, I regret to inform you that your brother has died as a result of a tragic motorcycle accident." It was at that moment that the Coleman family's world was turned upside down.

Now, I am sure that you have heard others who have faced unexpected, devastating tragedies express their disposition by saying things like, "It was so surreal. I couldn't believe it was happening to me." But what you have to understand is that for us it seemed as though history had forgotten that we had just gone through a similar scenario and now some error in the universe had us facing tragedy once again. We were still attempting to recuperate from dealing with the unexpected death of Reginald's wife Charnell, which had taken place only five months prior. So, surely this could not be happening to our family again. But the reality is that it was, and this time it was in an even greater magnitude. Reginald (affectionately known as Reggie) and Charnell (affectionately known as Charnie – pronounced Sharnell or Sharnie) were a young, absolutely gorgeous, vivacious and spirited couple. Reggie was only 27 at the time of his death and Charnie 29. Both of them were in the prime of their lives. They loved music and were heavily involved in the local Chicago music industry. Charnell was a dancer and a hair stylist who had just graduated from hair school. Reggie was pursuing his bachelor's degree in business and working diligently on his music career as an up and coming rap artist and producer.

No words can adequately describe Reggie. He was funny, cool, domineering yet easy-going, highly intelligent, super sarcastic, and proud, all wrapped up together. Reggie had already recorded a video and several songs and was becoming very well-known moving up the ranks and performing in venues with the likes of Kanye West and R. Kelley. What is significant to note however is that both Reggie and Charnell were born-again believers who just a few years prior had confessed Christ and were positioned to live a more committed life. They were members of our church who were making strides in becoming more devout in their faith every day. But in a five-month period of time, the both of them made their transition from earth into eternity, unexpectedly and tragic beyond all measure.

It was on the Saturday morning of October 4, 2008 that Charnell made her transition from this life. I'll

PRELUDE

never forget that day because I was about to return from St. Louis where I had been attending Joyce Meyer's annual Conference with my cousin Tina and some other women. We literally had just hung up the phone after being on our Saturday prayer call when the phone rang again. It was my husband John, calling to tell me that Reggie had just phoned him and said that Charnell was unresponsive and being transported to the hospital by ambulance. She was pronounced dead a little later the same morning.

Reggie recounting the events that ensued her passing, told us that morning he woke to a loud thump as he lay asleep in bed next to Charnell who also had been sleeping. He had heard a loud gasp and then all of a sudden she rolled out of the bed onto the floor and never woke up again. The medical examiner informed us all that she had died of a heart attack due to a blood clot. We all wondered in amazement how this could be. Charnell, not yet even thirty, had never been diagnosed with any heart problems and had no known serious illnesses. To our knowledge, she was perfectly healthy. In fact, out of all of us, she was considered to be the healthiest and had worked out regularly. So, how on earth could this happen?

For Reggie, now the single father of their three infant children: Ca'Koia, 4; Rain, 3; and Jream 10 months; though devastated by his wife's untimely death, was determined to move forward. He continued to pursue his degree, while making a living in the studio as well as pursuing his music career. Things were not the same by far, but he was focused on moving forward for the sake of his children. Now, fast forward five months later.

The day Reggie died seemed just like any other day. The only difference was that it was the middle of March and the weather was strikingly warm. Of course, we would often get these "Indian summers" in Chicago, but this first warm Saturday after a long harsh winter was significant. The whole Chicagoland was buzzing about the beautiful weather conditions and people were talking about doing this and that, whatever they could to get out and enjoy the beauty of the sun. Although Reggie was busy taking care of his business as usual, he had a quick errand to run and decided to saddle up his motorcycle, leaving his children at home with a friend, promising him he would be right back.

Reggie never came back. It was the last time that he would see his children and the last time he would ride his motorcycle. About a mile from his home, Reggie was hit head-on by a young man in a utility vehicle who tried to "beat" him making a left turn on a busy Chicago street. The man and his passengers were rumored to have been smoking marijuana and driving recklessly at the time of the accident. And

PRELUDE

despite a previous traffic violation, he was never convicted and neither did he serve any time. Again, how could this happen?

I believe that tragedy hits all of us at some point in our lives. And whether it was unexpected or something that you had a sense was inevitable, unless you have spiritually sound thinking, the devastation of it can become your demise.

This book is for everyone who has had to deal with a tragedy, and those who will eventually face one. You will be taught principles in the Word of God that you can use for effective intercession. You will receive prophetic insight into the spirit realm. You will be challenged to come up higher in your life. You will be motivated in the art of spiritual warfare. Most of all, you will learn how to pray from a realm in the spirit, where you will summon manifested breakthrough and get the results that you have desired!

OPENING PRAYER ACTIVATION

Father, I thank you that in the Name of Jesus everyone reading this book takes on the spirit of a Doer. I declare over them:

Not only will you read this book in its entirety, but as you read, the words on the pages will jump out and into your spirit bringing revelation, knowledge, insight and impartation. You will begin to immediately put what you are learning into action. Manifested breakthrough comes to you suddenly! Unanswered prayers spoken previously will begin to be answered. You will open up your mouth and pray the prayer strategies found here and encouragement will show up at your door step! You will pray new prayers in another dimension from another realm as the Holy Spirit begins to unction you.

The angels of the Lord will listen attentively to your requests and move speedily to bring the answer. You will see your miracles, manifestation and breakthrough. You will not cease to pray until what is revealed to you in the spirit becomes a reality in the natural. You are positioned to govern yourself as a Doer of the Word. The principles found here will begin to take over your life. You will begin to receive the engrafted Word of God and salvation and deliverance in every challenge will become your portion. The anointing to intercede and pray warfare prayers will increase over you. You will have insight into the spirit realm as one who has been taught of the Lord. This is your season to triumph over your enemy and move pass the failures that have held you back. So, arise and shine, for your light has come and the glory of the Lord is upon you, revealing to you new strategies, and positioning you as the conqueror that you have been destined to be!

SECTION ONE - THE GUIDE:
Discovering the DOERS Mindset to Get Results

CHAPTER ONE
Positioning for Prayer

In James 1:22, James, the younger brother of Jesus who became a leader in the Jerusalem church after Jesus' ministry on earth wrote these very powerful words, "But be ye doers of the word, and not hearers only, deceiving your own selves."

It is important to not only know what God's Word says, but it is much more important to obey it. We can measure the effectiveness of our church going, bible reading and scripture confessing by the effect it has on our behavior and attitudes. Romans 2:13 further reminds us that it is not merely listening to the law (God's Word) that makes us right with God, it is obeying that makes us right in His sight. (New Living Translation, paraphrased)

The more we mature in God, the more we develop a desire to conduct ourselves in accordance with His Word. This will require us opening ourselves and being teachable as well as trained in spiritual truths. When it comes to prayer, many have said that it is simply communicating with God. This is true in its "simplistic" form. However, there are degrees, dimensions and realms that we must learn to tap into in order to have more effective prayers. Just like we should not stop growing and learning after college, believers should understand that we should not stop at just knowing how to communicate with and petition God. There is more! And the only way we will achieve "the more" is if we hunger and thirst for it.

Prayers that get results require you to position yourself to pray from the realm of the Kingdom. The word kingdom literally means the King's domain. In the Greek it is *basileia* which means royal power, kingship, dominion and rule. It is not to be confused with an actual kingdom on earth but rather the right or authority to rule over a kingdom. In Genesis 1:26-27 we see that mankind was to have dominion. Dominion in the Hebrew comes from the word *mamlakah* which is the same word translated as kingdom. The "dom" syllable is in the word kingdom and dominion.

Both of these words indicate that you are in charge of something. You have authority over something. They mean leading, managing, and ruling over. Believers and particularly those who desire to be effective in prayer must answer the questions:

What are you leading?
What are you managing?
What are you ruling?

Positioning for Prayer

Knowing the correct answer is indication that they are positioned to get results. According to Genesis, the answer to these questions is simply creation or the earth. God has called us to take dominion in the earth. This will require us understanding that we are kings in the world and priests in the church.

When we are acting as priests we are interceding, standing in the gap and petitioning God. When we are acting as kings we are calling those things that be not as though they were; decreeing, declaring, binding, loosing and serving the devil his eviction papers. Therefore, we must pray prayers that are emanating from the realm of heaven. We must make sure that we are praying from our kingly position and not just our priestly position.

The Priestly Position

This is the position in which you and I act as the intercessors on earth pleading our cause, petitioning and praying for assistance here on earth.

Our priestly duties include our church attendance, our worship and prayer life, and our service to others. The language of the priest consists of asking, seeking and knocking. **From this position we look up to the Father.**

The Kingly Position

- The kingly position is a place in which we are seated with Christ Jesus as a joint heir.

- In this place we are looking down on our situations and decreeing what needs to take place.
- It is a position of authority, kingship, rule and dominance.
- It is not a position where we are asking.
- It is not a position where we are petitioning.
- It is a position where we have been given the right to call those things that be not as though they were. (Romans 4:17)

When a king makes a decree it becomes law. It must be carried out by all those that are in the Kingdom. When you and I pray from our kingly position, the angels in the Kingdom must hearken to the voice of God's Word spoken through us. They are our ministering spirits and just like the servants that minister and wait on a king, our angels are waiting to minister and bring us what we declare.

To truly understand our position as a king, we must look closely at excerpts from the letter that Paul wrote to the church of Ephesus in Ephesians, Chapter 1:

1. **Ephesians 1:3**
   Blessed be the God and Father of our Lord Jesus Christ, who hath blessed us with all spiritual blessings in **heavenly places** in Christ:

2. **Ephesians 1:20**
   Which he wrought in Christ, when he raised him from the dead, and set him at his own right hand in the **heavenly places**,

3. **Ephesians 2:6**
   And hath raised us up together, and made us sit together in **heavenly places** in Christ Jesus:

4. **Ephesians 3:10**
   To the intent that now unto the principalities and powers in **heavenly places** might be known by the church the manifold wisdom of God...

Remember, a king does not have to ask for anything, he simply decrees. A king does not have to seek for anything, he simply has someone bring it to him. A king does not even open his own door. Someone goes before him and opens it up for him.

Oftentimes, believers get the two roles mixed up. So we attend church and we walk around our house decreeing and declaring things over others. We try and rule over others when we should be operating in the position of a fellow servant, worshipper and mediator. Then, when we go out into the world and operate, we are to act as a king. It is then that we decree, declare, occupy and take possession of what belongs to us.

From this position as a king we look down on everything which includes our problems. They are no longer governing over us but we have authority over them.

The kingly and priestly anointings are like two sides of a coin. Jesus was the lion and the lamb. He was full of grace and full of truth. We are kings and priests!

Praying from a Realm

Dictionary.com defines realm as: a royal domain; kingdom; the region, sphere, or domain within which anything occurs, prevails, or dominates; the special province or field of something or someone.

A realm is a set place in which you operate. There are people that live in the realm of wealth and there are people that live in the realm of poverty. As believers we are to live in the realm of the Kingdom. Consequently, all of our needs are met in this realm and there is no poverty.

From this realm or region, we are operating in a dimension of affluence and influence. We are praying from a place of rule and authority. With this attitude and understanding we are able to influence the mountain that we have been called to rule in the world as outlined in 1975 by Bill Bright, founder of *Campus Crusade,* and Loren Cunningham, founder of *Youth With a Mission.* The Lord simultaneously revealed to both of them that believers needed to impact the nations by becoming influencers within the seven spheres or mountains of society: business, government, media, arts and entertainment, education, family and religion.

CHAPTER TWO
Passionately Pursuing Your Promise

James 5:16 states that the effective, fervent prayer of the righteous man avails much! It's about time that your prayers brought you results every time! Getting results from your prayers will require a passionate pursuit of your promise.

Your prayer results are going to come as a product of your passionate pursuit. The apathetic, pessimistic attitude will not work when it comes to getting your prayer results. You are going to have to retrain your brain, equip your emotions and increase your desire to see manifested change in your situation.

Your promise is what the Word of God says belongs to you. Your promise is your inheritance, your birthright, your due blessing! Although your promise belongs to you, there is a process of occupying that must take place in order to get it manifested. It's like receiving a gift. You have to open the gift to access the blessing in it. Likewise, your passionate pursuit of your promise will help you access what already belongs to you.

"And he called his ten servants, and delivered them ten pounds, and said unto them, **Occupy** till I come." Luke 19:13

Pursuing your promise is like an army from one kingdom subduing the army of another kingdom. Although the conquering army has declared victory, there are still areas in which enemy forces often occupy that must now be occupied by the conquering army. There must be an aggressive advancement into those areas to secure, possess and take dominion. Likewise, your passionate pursuit of your promise will help you access what already belongs to you.

In the fall of 1990 after the United States invaded Iraq, just a few months later in early 1991, it quickly declared a victory. However, years and years later much resistance in various territories of Iraq required that US army forces continue to go into those regions and occupy them until the enemy forces were rendered ineffective. As believers, we must learn how to occupy enemy territory with fervency and focus. For the Kingdom of Heaven suffers violence and the violent take it by force.

When the scriptures refer to the Kingdom of God it means God's rule over all creation; it's His sovereignty in full manifestation; God's rule. However, when we see the Kingdom of heaven in the scriptures, it is God's rule through man in the earth. When John the Baptist came to the earth he began to declare that people repent because the Kingdom of heaven was at hand. Jesus entering into the earth, dying, rising and gaining victory over death, hell and the grave would bring back to man his authority to rule that he had lost to Satan.

That's why Matthew 11:12 says, "And from the days of John the Baptist until now the kingdom of heaven suffers violence, and the violent take it by force." Another version states:

Matthew 11:12 – "And from the days of John the Baptist until the present time, the kingdom of heaven has endured violent assault, and violent men seize it by force [as a precious prize--a [a]share in the heavenly kingdom is sought with most ardent zeal and intense exertion]." The Amplified Bible

The problem with many believers is that they are standing inside of the door of salvation still shouting because they got into the Kingdom of Heaven. They have settled at the door and are refusing to access the other dimensions in the Kingdom.

The Kingdom of Heaven is the place in space that God has given His children grace! God has placed so much of the responsibility of the rulership of earth on His sons and daughters until He has chosen to limit Himself to only ruling through us. It's like the father that gives his children the authority to operate his business. The father goes away and has now left the children with the responsibility of making the decisions and carrying out the duties of the business. Because the father is not physically at the business and has therefore chosen to limit himself in the running of the business, the customers now have to deal with the children. Although, the failure or success of the day to day business transactions will now be determined by the management of the children, the overall wellness and sustainability of the business will be determined by the integrity of the father, the foundation he has established and his eventual intervention if need be. We must constantly request that God intervene in our earthly affairs.

Likewise, the Father has given His children the opportunity to run His business affairs here on earth, and the only way we will successfully do this is by occupying territory that the enemy has possessed thus far; taking it by force.

<u>The Body</u>

As believers we must remember that we are the body of Christ. Think about it. Have you ever seen a head walking around taking care of business? I cannot think of a single time when I've seen a head bouncing around taking care of business! The head needs the body to perform its actions! Jesus Christ rules through us in the earth realm!

If your arms, your hands, legs, feet or various parts of your body do not have the ability to move, they would be considered paralyzed. As a matter of fact, you may even be deemed incapacitated. If your body parts are not able to function as they should it could even be concluded that they are "good for nothing."

It is time for the malfunctioning parts of the body to be evicted, so that the healthy body of Christ can arise to possess our promise. Unfortunately, broken and out of order is how many people in the body of Christ look. There is a lack of aggression, little momentum, no occupying, and limited fruit manifesting in their lives. They are like that light that has been hidden, instead of the city that should be on the hill. We are the salt that cannot afford to lose our savor. If we do, then we are good for nothing but to be trampled upon. (Matthew 5:13-15)

Violent People

The Gospel according to Matthew is such a beautiful illustration of the Kingdom of Heaven and the Kingdom of God. It reminds us of God's sovereignty and our sonship in relationship to His sovereignty. God's Kingdom does not operate like this world's system. God's Kingdom has an entirely different order and protocol. God's Kingdom is a kingdom based on His principles. It requires that those that are its citizens live their lives by faith.

The Amplified Bibles says the Kingdom of Heaven has endured violent assault and the violent take it by force. Don't think that you can just blab it and grab it; or just do nothing and your prayers will manifest in the by and by. No, it's going to take an aggressive act on your part. It's going to require unfailing faith!

Many believers make it into the door of the Kingdom. Jesus is the door so they accept Him as Lord and Savior. However, they don't realize that because of Jesus' finished work on the cross they have access to all the benefits in the Kingdom. In the Kingdom there are rooms of healing, levels of prosperity, atmospheres of peace, dimensions of joy, and so on. Many believers are just glad that they made it in and so they just shout at the door not realizing that there are so many other levels and dimensions of blessings waiting on them throughout the Kingdom. I believe it was the late, great Dr. Myles Munroe that taught this concept of believers sitting at the door and not accessing all of what God has in store for them in the Kingdom. We cannot afford to just sit at the door of the Kingdom when there is territory that must be occupied.

<u>Dining at the Table</u>

Imagine your boss wants to do something nice for you, so he makes accommodations for you and a loved one to dine at an exclusive five-star restaurant. Your bill will be paid in full and you have been given the authority to order whatever it is you desire. The night of your reservations finally arrives. You and your guest drive up to the restaurant and are escorted in by a very polite and helpful valet. The handsome well-groomed host greets you at the door. The room is filled with the aroma of seasonings emanating from marinated dishes being prepared in the kitchen.

As you look around, people are quietly talking and laughing, seemingly having the time of their lives. This is the type of dining experience that you had only dreamed of and now the time has finally come when you can experience it. The host beckons you to follow him as there is a special area in the restaurant reserved just for you. But wait, there is one problem; you are so mesmerized with the fact that you are surrounded by such opulence and were able to finally dine at the restaurant that you just stand there in total adoration and bliss. You never make the extra steps to go and sit at your table. So the waiter never gets an opportunity to take your order, and you never take the opportunity to select from a menu of exquisite delicacies and taste the food prepared by one of the finest chefs in the world. Perhaps this scenario sounds a little exaggerated, but the fact is there are many Christians who settle for just making it into heaven, but they never sit down at the Master's table to dine.

Salvation & Redemption

Jesus saves us but our redemption is based on operating in and practicing the principles found in the

Word of God.

As referenced previously, Luke 19:11-27 outlines a parable of what the Kingdom is like.

A nobleman went away to a distant place to obtain a kingdom but left his servants with the means to conduct his business until he returned. When he returned they were all summoned to give an account of their productivity. The first servant had doubled his lord's money and because he was faithful over a little, his lord made him ruler over much. The second servant came and had produced not as much as the first but he did produce and therefore was rewarded likewise. The last servant comes and hasn't produced anything and that which he had been given is taken away and given to the first man.

This last servant can be likened to the person that just stands inside of the door of salvation, shouting, praising God and on their way to heaven. However, because they are not occupying the promises that belong to them, they are often living like "hell." Diseases, debt, depression, and discouragement meet them on a daily basis. So, to escape from this, every now and then they have to get their "shout on" knowing that soon and very soon they are going to see the King and thus end their misery. The only solace that they have is in knowing that one day in the sweet by and by it will all be over. Jesus will return to swoop them up and take them to a heavenly place of peace and tranquility. There will be no more tears.

But haven't they forgotten the lesson that Jesus teaches in this parable? Those that take what they have and produce with it will be given more, but those that do not produce will be required to give even that which they have.

Notice that in verse 27, the story also says that there were citizens that refused to even serve the nobleman and they were condemned to death. This represents the people that will never come into the Kingdom because they refuse to accept Jesus as Lord.

There are 3 types of people I have identified in this story:

1) The ones that refuse to enter into the Kingdom
2) The ones that enter in but stay at the door
3) The ones that enter and ascend to new levels and dimensions, obtaining all that God has for them because they desire to be productive.

I believe that we determine which one of those people that we will be, based on our choice to pursue or not to pursue.

CHAPTER THREE
Potency & Power

Prayers that get results require potency and power!

Acts 1:8 says that after the Holy Ghost has come upon you, you shall receive power and you shall be witnesses unto God. We have everything we need to manifest the results we want. However, we have to live in the realm of the Kingdom.

Remember the realm of the Kingdom is never broke, it's never in recession and there is no sickness, sin or disease existing there.

<u>Personal Pentecost</u>

Jude 1:20 tells us to build ourselves up by praying in the Holy Ghost. We have to do this because of this fallen world that we live in, and because demonic forces are consistently trying to beat us down. As we build ourselves up, that power makes us witnesses for Jesus. It causes us to put Him on display and bring glory to God!

The book of Acts, Chapter 2, says that after that day had fully come is when the Holy Spirit came. He could not come until it was the right time. The word "fully" implies maturity. The Holy Spirit has not manifested in some people fully because of a lack of maturity. That's why it is important that we don't grieve the Holy Spirit. Just like it is a challenge for you to help someone that grieves you, it hinders the Holy Spirit from helping us when we grieve Him.

We want answered prayer, we want revival, Pentecost, a move of God to take place in our lives, yet often times we don't want to grow up enough for it to happen. The prefix *pente* means "the best of" and "on top". If we want the best of life, we can have it, but we have got to remember that it is going to "cost" us something; Pentecost. Power costs! Ask your local electric company.

Understand, that they were not in the upper room with hidden agendas or secret motives. They were waiting with expectation for that day to fully come. Just like stocks, bonds and trust funds, we have to fully mature in order to get the full benefit of our walk with the Holy Ghost. When we do we'll have our Pentecost experience. *Pente*: the best of, on top!

Fuel for the Fire

Mature believers know the importance of walking in love and forgiveness. We need fuel for our faith which is what gives us the power to pray prayers that get results. Galatians 5:6 reminds us that our faith works by our love. We must have a passion and strong desire to see what we are praying for come to pass. We must take a pass on passivity. Prayers that get results require a pass on being passive. Although you should choose your battles, on some things you can't afford to just sit back and let them happen as they will! You cannot afford to be meek and mild when it comes to your destiny!

Joshua 1:8 says that YOU become prosperous and successful when YOU speak God's Word and YOU do God's Word. We must act like God and 2/3 of God's name is GO! God wants us to 'occupy' which means to do business! We must be about the business of advancing God's Kingdom in the earth.

Speak Up

In Numbers, Chapter 1, there is a brief story mentioned about the five daughters of Zelophehad. These women refused to settle. In a culture, where women were treated less than men and often as the property of men, they stood boldly and requested the inheritance of their deceased father. The Lord agreed that the inheritance belonged to them and commanded Moses to release it. What do you imagine would have happened if they were passive and did not speak up?

These women believed their father left them loaded. Our Father has left us loaded! As believers, we have to embrace this revelation—that God has left us loaded—and behave as if we believe it…claiming our inheritance.

Stand Up

In the book of John, Chapter 5, the man at the pool of Bethesda sat there in that familiar place while he suffered with an infirmity for thirty-eight years. Bethesda means house of mercy and flowing water. At this pool there were five porches. Five represents the number of grace. This porch provided shelter from inclement weather as all those who were impotent, blind, lame and withered waited for an angel to stir the waters so they could jump in and receive a miracle of healing. They were in expectation, but the first point to be noted is that the only one that would get their miracle would be the one that jumped in first. Therefore, they could not afford to be passive.

The second observation that should be noted is that Jesus showed up and asked the man if he was willing to be made whole. Jesus tapped into the inner passion of the man and addressed his will. This stirred the man's faith and when Jesus told him to "Arise and take up his bed and walk," it connected with the man's passion. This man left his comfortable place (took up his bed) and he walked out of his situation. He and the others had become comfortable on those porches because they were sheltered from the weathers of life. How often have you become comfortable in your miserable and less than perfect situations? Cut the comfortable out of your life!

- Pass on Passivity by refusing to give into that which is comfortable.
- Pass on Passivity by being willing to challenge the current system.
- Pass on Passivity by not believing that God wants you to settle.
- If the enemy says you can't, that's a sure sign that you can! Don't pass out!
- If the enemy says you are not, you better believe you are! Don't pass your power!

Remember that everything God does starts in seed form. There is a process. Don't be weary in well-doing during the process. Stand up and stay up!

Stay Up

About a decade ago, with the Lord's leading, my husband and I set out to pioneer a church. Pioneering a church is different from a church plant. A church plant is when, with the help of others—usually a group or at the very least a more seasoned spiritual advisor—you start (plant) a new church. Usually there is spiritual, relational, and even financial support that is given to help build the ministry. To pioneer a church however is a different dynamic. This usually means that you found it, fund it and normally are the first in that particular area to do so. It's like building a house from the ground up instead of just renovating something that is already there.

At our launch service two people became members. It was a very humble beginning. About a year into the ministry we began to experience challenges we had never experienced in the history of our lives and our ten-year marriage at the time. My husband began to develop a severe hernia problem which eventually led to major surgery. Due to expenses we had discontinued our very good insurance and were still in the market for something more affordable. After all, neither of us had ever been hospitalized or had any health problems.

The surgery went okay but the weeks of recovery, and enduring the pain and side effects was excruciating. Our ministry had begun to experience some growth. However, in a time when we needed them the most some of the very people that called him "father" were the very ones that started up strife and left the church. Instead of throwing in the towel, we said that we would not give up. Not too long after that as already mentioned in the Introduction, Reggie & Charnell passed away and we took on the responsibility of raising their three small children. Our worlds at that point TOTALLY changed. However, because my husband had experienced his share of tragedy in childhood, he had made up in his mind years before that he was "Still going to do it!" This became the official motto of our household. We've got the t-shirt literally to back it up!

Potency & Power

If we are not careful oftentimes, when it takes a while for our breakthroughs to manifest, we can find ourselves making statements like, "God told me to do something else," as though God is bipolar, or schizophrenic and prone to sudden changes of heart. We must remember that the failure is never in God. It is in our inability to be active in doing what He told us to do...no matter the obstacles.

Fast forward ten years into starting our church. We now have our own building, paid in full. We are pastoring an intimate yet powerful congregation. Our social media, local, national and even international influence is expanding. We were determined to speak up, stand up and stay up! When you choose to take a pass on being passive, tap into your potency and power and persevere in prayer you get results!

CHAPTER FOUR
Perseverance & Persistence

"Then said he unto me, Fear not, Daniel: for from the first day that thou didst set thine heart to understand, and to chasten thyself before thy God, thy words were heard, and I am come for thy words. But the prince of the kingdom of Persia withstood me one and twenty days: but, lo, Michael, one of the chief princes, came to help me; and I remained there with the kings of Persia. Now I am come to make thee understand what shall befall thy people in the latter days: for yet the vision is for many days." Daniel 10:12-14

When it comes to getting results and answers to your prayers or breakthrough in whatever you are trying to accomplish, perseverance and persistency will be required. In Daniel, Chapter 10 (read it in its entirety), there are some lessons regarding prayer and spiritual warfare that we can learn.

- Daniel was totally committed to getting his breakthrough and his prayer answered.
- He was willing to do whatever it took both spiritually and naturally.
- He denied and deprived himself.

- The angel was sent on a mission specifically to answer Daniel's prayer.
- When his breakthrough came, he was commanded to stand again.
- Daniel's prayer was heard the first day his heart desired to understand and his will humbled itself in denial.
- The angel was coming the first day, but ended up in warfare for 21 days with the ruling spirit over the region of Persia. (When your heart and disposition is right, the answer is released immediately.)
- There are demonic forces set in place that are attempting to keep your breakthrough from happening.
- You must persevere until the answer comes and the breakthrough manifests.

Prayers that get results require perseverance and persistence. Therefore:

- YOU MUST NOT FAINT - If you faint in the day of adversity your strength is small! "If you fall to pieces in a crisis, there wasn't much to you in the first place!" (Proverbs 24:10, The Message)
- YOU MUST NOT BE DOUBLE MINDED - You can't be double-minded! A double-minded man is unstable in all of his ways, let

not that man (or woman) think they'll obtain anything from God! James 1:8
- YOU MUST NOT SPEAK NEGATIVELY - Negotiations between angelic and demonic forces are taking place in the heavenly realms regarding your prayers, but the minute you speak negatively, you give the devil permission to intercept. The angel of the Lord is traveling through realms and dimensions to bring breakthrough. But he has opposition because Ephesians 2:2 says that Satan is the prince and the power of the air. He is waiting to intercept your breakthrough.

Demonic Interception = Skid Marks in the Sky

Delve with me and open up to the canvas of your imagination. I believe there are skid marks being made all over the spirit realm constantly. These skid marks represent angels who were in flight bringing answers to our prayers, but were stopped suddenly in their tracks because of demonic intervention and/or negative words spoken by us.

Imagine for a moment how activity in the spirit realm might look. We pray a prayer. The angel takes our prayer to heaven to receive an answer from God. Whenever we send our prayers up to God, He always hears us and answers our petitions as long as it is according to His will. (1 John 5:14-15) His promises are "Yes" and "Amen." (2 Corinthians 1:20) The angel is on his way back to us with the "Yes" answers to our promises. However, he runs into opposition in the spirit realm from opposing angelic forces and a battle ensues.

Meanwhile, receiving our answer is prolonged, and instead of continuing to pray and stand in faith we begin to get negative, complain and give up hope of having our prayers answered. Our negative disposition and communication is witnessed by the demonic forces assigned to our lives. They take this communication and use it to work against us receiving our answer. Instead of us reinforcing our prayers with faith and positive confessions, we are now causing them to be hindered. In the meantime, the angel that carries the answer to our prayer is in warfare and in need of assistance. Because we are no longer standing in faith and sending prayers up, heaven is not getting the signal that our answer has not yet been received. Therefore, reinforcements from heaven are not being sent to assist the angel with our answer.

A real life example of this can be seen in 2015, when the Seattle Seahawks played the New England patriots in Super Bowl XLIX. Seattle coach Pete Caroll called the play for the ball to be thrown with twenty seconds left in the game. It was then intercepted by Malcolm Butler in the end zone giving New England a 28-24 Super Bowl victory. Tom

Perseverance & Persistence

Brady the Patriots quarterback was quoted as saying, "It was the perfect play at the perfect time." (CBS News)

Your Mouth, Your Movement

Demonic forces are strategizing against us and waiting for the perfect opportunity to hinder our prayers. Every time we give up, lose hope and speak negatively, we provide that perfect time for them to make their move. Demonic forces often intercept our breakthroughs because of the negative words we have spoken. Here is another scenario to consider:

Your AM Prayer:

"Lord, Your Word has declared that by Jesus' stripes I was already healed. Father, You said that He who knew no sin became sin for me, who knew no righteousness and now I am called righteous in Christ Jesus. Lord, Your Word says in 3 John 2 that I am to prosper and be in good health even as my soul prospers. So, Father I believe you for the healing. I believe that I don't have to accept sickness in my body."

You go throughout your day, and then all of a sudden you begin to feel the symptoms of the sickness. They become so unbearable that you can hardly work. Eventually, you have to leave work, go home and lie down. Your loved ones check on you and then it happens…:

Your PM Confession:

> "I am in so much pain. I feel like I am going to die. I don't know what I'm going to do. It hurts here, here and here. And Lord knows I can't take too much of this."

You have just given the kingdom of darkness both the right and the room to intercept that prayer breakthrough for healing that was on its way to your doorstep.

"For verily I say unto you, that whosoever shall say unto this mountain, be thou removed, and be thou cast into the sea; and shall not doubt in his heart, but shall believe that those things which he saith shall come to pass; he shall have whatsoever he saith." Mark 11:23

"For by thy words thou shalt be justified, and by thy words thou shalt be condemned." Matthew 12:37

There is a television commercial that plays quite often which depicts a lady talking about her condition with diabetes. Constantly throughout the commercial she repeats the phrase, "My diabetes…" As believers we cannot hold claim to anything that does not align with the finished work of Jesus on the

Perseverance & Persistence

cross. The bible says that by Jesus' stripes we "were" healed. (1 Peter 2:24) Either we are or we are not. We cannot be both.

Don't Miss Your Breakthrough

Angelic and demonic forces understand that our words are spiritual and the spirit realm is governed by laws. Although, we humans often break laws and don't think anything of it, angels and demons understand their importance and base their activity on them. So, the enemy has been looking for a legal right to intercept your breakthrough and you give it to him when you decide to give into negative communication from your mouth.

I can imagine that some believers' angels are frustrated! I can imagine them saying, "Man she did it again, she did it again! She opened up her mouth and caused her blessing to be intercepted." I can imagine those angels standing before the throne room again pleading with the Father to assign them to someone else, "Lord please assign me to Brother John. I want to see some manifested breakthrough in a believer's life! I'm tired of all this work for nothing!" As funny as it might seem, many of us cause our breakthroughs to be intercepted because of the negative words that we speak out of our mouths.

Remember, the devil is the prince and the power of the air, so he has jurisdiction in the airways and monitors what is going on there. Immediately, when we put something into the atmosphere with our words, those demonic forces assigned to our lives check to see if they have a legal right (an open door, room to work) to intercept it. The minute we open up our mouths we are either empowering the angelic army of God to work on our behalf or empowering the demonic army of Satan to work against us.

Don't Miss Your Opportunity

"But I will tarry at Ephesus until Pentecost. For a great door and effectual is opened unto me, and there are many adversaries." 1 Corinthians 16:8-10

A great door and effectual means a door of opportunity for doing effective work was opened to Paul. Oftentimes, the breakthrough comes but we miss the opportunity to receive it because we don't want to persevere through the opposition. The opportunity comes with opposition. Persevere and be persistent!

CHAPTER FIVE
Performing the Principles

Prayers that get results require performance of a principle that will bring breakthrough to the particular situation we are praying for. We have often missed out on our blessings because we have been all talk and no walk!

Salvation brings us into the Kingdom but redemption gives us access to the Kingdom's resources. Salvation secures your eternal standing in Heaven, but redemption relates to your temporal walk on the earth. We live a redeemed life by practicing the principles of Yeshua. A principle is defined as a rule or a code of conduct. Whenever Jesus healed, He would give an instruction that a person needed to follow. However, many believers get healed and then go back and do the same thing they were doing before.

Consider this scenario: A person with diabetes goes to a miracle service, gets healed and after church goes to the local 'all you can eat' buffet and piles their plate up with numerous entrees and all kinds of delicacies. Many believers stand in healing lines and receive a miracle, but then they go about participating in the same activities that made them sick.

The principles of God govern the universe and they affect everything around us. The word of God is His government on the earth and we are His representatives assigned to legislate and carry out His governmental mandates. We are to represent, that is re-present, Jesus in the earth. Unfortunately, God's people seem to forget to operate in the principles more than worldly people. It often seems that the people in the world are wiser than those that are of the light. (Luke 16:8)

Think about it, the 2006 best-selling self-help book *The Secret* became an overnight hit, due to the fact it taught people about the law of attraction and positive thinking. The book explained how people could create life-changing results such as increased happiness, health, and wealth. The irony is this "secret" was never a secret in the first place, because it has already been clearly communicated over and over again in the bible. For instance, here are some examples from scripture that *The Secret* communicates through its teachings:

If you want to attract friends, you need to be friendly. (Proverbs 18:24)

If you want to be in good health, it starts with your mind. (3 John 2)

If you can believe, all things are possible. (Mark 9:23)

Performing the Principles

If you ask, you will receive. If you seek, you will find. If you knock, it will be opened. (Matthew 7:8)

A life of abundance has been promised for you. (John 10:10)

As a man thinks, so is he. (Proverbs 23:7)

You will reap whatever you sow. (Galatians 6:7)

Everything you need is available. (2 Corinthians 9:8)

Think good thoughts. (Philippians 4:8)

Out of a good heart comes good things. (Luke 6:35)

God just doesn't want to heal us. He wants to make us whole. (Luke 17:11-19) Wholeness is a manifestation of redemption. Wholeness is making sure you stay away from that which makes you broken. In John 5:14, Jesus told the man who had been infirmed for 38 years, but then was healed at His Word, to go and sin no more, unless a greater thing should come upon him. Although, the man had been healed, he needed to walk in wholeness by practicing the principles and staying away from the sinful activity that opened the door to the sickness in the first place. It should be noted here that all sickness and suffering is not due to some sin we have committed, but in this case it was.

You live a redeemed life by doing. Let the redeemed of the Lord say so. (Psalm 107:2) There's something you have to do. You have to practice the principles of Jesus.

The bible is filled with principles to live by. There are at least six hundred and thirteen principles and Ten Commandments. Remember that Jesus didn't come to destroy the law He came to fulfill it. So, Jesus came to give us the authority back to live the redeemed lifestyle. We were trying to live in our flesh before, but now we have the Holy Spirit to help us live out the principles. It is not by might nor by power, but by God's Spirit. (Zechariah 4:6)

Some of the most important principles that we need to practice to see our prayers manifest, are:

The Praise Principle

As believers, this is something that should be automatic to us. Psalm 3:1 says, "It's comely to the upright." It's befitting us. Praise looks good on the believer! It's what we are supposed to do!

Our praise shuts the mouth of the enemy. During warfare Israel was commanded to send Judah (praise) first into the battle. (Judges 1:2, 20:18) It establishes a stronghold against your enemies to silence them. It binds the devil up and shuts him up. He walks around as a roaring lion, but our praise puts a fist in his mouth. Releasing your praise clears the path in the heavenlies for your angel to get through.

God inhabits the praises of His people. When God shows up, the devil, sickness, and disease has got to go. Stay in an attitude of gratitude to receive the magnitude of the manifestation you are looking for!

The Paradigm Principle

There has to be a paradigm shift! You must practice the principle of renewing your mind:

Romans 12:1-2: "I beseech you therefore, brethren, by the mercies of God, that ye present your bodies a living sacrifice, holy, acceptable unto God, which is your reasonable service. And be not conformed to this world: but be ye transformed by the renewing of your mind, that ye may prove what is that good, and acceptable, and perfect, will of God."

Matthew 9:17 says, "Neither do men put new wine into old bottles: else the bottles break, and the wine runneth out, and the bottles perish: but they put new wine into new bottles, and both are preserved." This is talking about making a paradigm shift.

Let's look at the process of making new wine skins according to Jewish Culture. First of all, you will notice that the old wine skins were not just thrown out. Aren't you so glad that God didn't just throw you out? But there is a process. You may be being processed.

1. Take the old wine skin and take the spout off and TURN IT INSIDE OUT. The new mindset will require us living from the inside out and no longer the outside in. We have to live a life that is dictated by the Spirit and not by our fleshly desires.

2. Next in the process they would take a double-edged knife and SLICE OFF THE LUMPS on the inside of the wine skin. Now this is the pruning and purging process. Some beliefs, attitudes, and people in our life have to be cut off or left behind. (Pruning and purging is so that we can bring forth more fruit).

3. Thirdly, they would put the newly smooth bag, still inside out, in a river of running water. The old wine skin is soaked in the river until the skin becomes soft again. SOAKED IN WATER (representing the Holy Spirit and Jesus the Word). Notice it wasn't stagnant water but it was water that was moving. It was water that was going places. The Holy Spirit will groom our attitudes and motives by bringing to our remembrance the word of God and by convicting us when we are not on

Performing the Principles

the right track. Our prayer should be, "Lord, sanctify me with truth. Your Word is truth. (John 17:17) We need to soak so much in the Word until it cleanses our minds and washes away every thought contrary to God's plan for our lives.

4. In the next step, the person would take oil and rub it into the wine skin until it was saturated. (SATURATED IN OIL) Saturation in the Word of God and in the presence of God increases the anointing on our lives. It is the anointing that destroys the yoke. This repetitious conduct of continuously saturating ourselves with the Word and in God's presence through worship, changes us into a new person. Our old garments are gone away. (Ephesians 4:22-24, Job 29:14, Isaiah 61:10) We maintain a relationship where we are in constant communication and spending time with the Lord.

5. In the final stage of creating a new wine skin, the wine skin is turned right side out and a NEW SPOUT IS PUT ON ITS MOUTH. You now have a new vocabulary. You are no longer from the We-be-not Tribe but now you speak the vocabulary of the We-Be-Well-

Able tribe! (I will elaborate more on these two groups of people in Chapter Six.)

The Pay Principle

This is the last and most important principle that we need to understand and operate in. If you want to grow; you've got to sow. You can't receive anything in life without sowing a seed. God wanted an earthly family so He sowed the seed of His Son. (John 3:16) Prayers that get results require sowing a seed to reap a harvest of breakthrough.

To the natural man, sowing seeds to get breakthroughs might sound foolish or even heretical. However, this principle is practiced many times in the Word.

Kingdom Concepts are the Opposite of Earthly Concepts

- If you want to gain life, you must be willing to lose your life.
- If you want to be great, you've got to serve.
- If you want to be lifted up, you've got to humble yourself.
- If you want to increase, you must decrease.
- If you want to have, you must give.

YOUR SEED IS YOUR KEY TO BREAKTHROUGH PRAYER! Everything God does, He does in seed form.

Luke 6:38 reminds us that in order to receive we must first give. But when you give it's not coming back to you the same. It's coming back to you multiplied. It is coming back pressed down, shaken together and running over! The bible also teaches that if we sow the wind, we will reap the whirlwind. (Hosea 8:7)

CHAPTER SIX
The Prescription for Your Pain

Even as a young girl attending worship services, I was extremely amazed at the depth of revelation and insight often orated from the men and women of God standing before me. Among many things, the Word of God has the power to inspire, guide, encourage, inform and deliver us. It also has the power to produce the results that we need in life.

Just like a tool that can be misused and not yield maximum results because of improper handling, the Word of God is often misused and even overlooked when it comes to applying it to our lives. Jesus said "if" we would abide in Him and His words would abide in us, we could ask whatever we wanted and it would be given to us. (John 15:7) When the Word becomes a part of you that means it cannot be separated from you. It goes from being a thought and an affirmation, to becoming you; just like how the Word (Jesus) became flesh and manifested in the earth, we manifest the Word when it becomes a part of us. (John 1) Now that the Word has become you, it superimposes all natural circumstances. Truth (the Word) which is eternal, now begins to overcome the facts (temporal reality).

<u>Standing in the Word</u>

When the Word of God is a part of you, it can't be separated from you. When you begin to confess it to the point of it abiding in you, it goes from thought to affirmation. When you begin to affirm and believe the words that you are speaking, your behavior begins to line up with it. Remember that the Word of God and the promises of God are already a reality in the spirit realm, but you must speak them into the natural realm. By faith you are framing your world with your words. (Hebrews 11:3) Remember that the earth is voice-activated, because in the beginning God spoke it into existence, "Let there be..." (Genesis 1)

The words that God spoke carried the faith that caused creation to come into existence. Likewise, the words that you speak create images that you eventually act upon and manifest. The more you speak what you believe, the bigger that image gets. The bigger the image gets, the more you will speak about it. The more you speak about it the bigger it gets. The bigger it gets, the more it becomes a part of you. It is now engrafted to you and engrained within you. It is you and now it must manifest in the natural realm. (John 6:63)

The Prescription for Your Pain

Order Your Conversation

Psalm 50:23 reminds us that we are to order our conversation in the right direction because it determines our salvation and the degree of deliverance we can walk in.

We can see the opposite of this working in Numbers Chapter 13, when twelve of the best men from the tribes of the Israelites went to scout out the land of Canaan. Only two came back with a positive attitude and faith-filled words. The rest of them confessed, "We be not able to go up against the people…" (verse 31). Caleb tried to ward off their negative report by confessing, "We are well able to overcome it, (verse 30) but he and Joshua were the only two that trusted in what God had already spoken. It is time for the church to rid itself of the negative "Ebonics" spirit that declares, "We be not…" and confess, "We are well able to lay hold of all of the promises of God!"

The Word can become so much a part of you until like Jesus, it is you. It is your constant conversation and it begins to superimpose everything else that comes against you. Truth begins to overtake facts. This is going to require a humbling of the heart and putting off all natural reasoning. The seed of the Word can't enter into a closed (prideful) heart. Therefore, we must receive with meekness, the engrafted Word which is able to save our souls. (James 1:21)

This will require a broken and a contrite heart in order for the seed of the Word to get in.

"...A broken and contrite heart, God, will not despise." (Psalm 51:17)

Psalm 107:20 says, God sent His Word and healed them and delivered them. Notice the scripture did not say "to" heal them. It said "and." It was a done deal.

The Doctor, The Prescription, The Pharmacist

In Luke 4:18-19, Jesus made a profound declaration in the synagogue when He revealed His purpose for being on the earth. He was sent by the Father to set the captives free. The earth had a problem and Jesus was the solution. He was just what our Father, the Doctor ordered. And although Jesus is not physically here in human form anymore, He is here manifesting through His Word. (John 1:1-2, 14)

His Word is the prescription that we need to take for the "sick" situations in our lives. Just like we call on the doctor when we are sick, we need to call on the Name of the Lord for there is where our help comes from. (Psalm 121) God is our doctor. The doctor prescribes us the Word (Jesus) to cure our disease. However, just like a natural prescription, we often

The Prescription for Your Pain

don't know how to go about taking that which is prescribed to us, so we need to consult with a pharmacist to assist us in our process of application. The Holy Spirit, like a pharmacist, will guide us in the proper application of the Word.

One key thing that you must remember, is when the doctor (Our Father) prescribes your prescription (the Word), your mother can't take it for you. Your spouse can't take it for you; your best friend, pastor or prayer partner can't take it for you. That prescription has to get down on the inside of you to bring you deliverance. The prayers of others are essential and can even influence our situations. However, the only way for you to get well and receive your breakthrough is for you to take the prescription. You have to believe that the Word works and you have to open up your mouth and declare it.

<u>"Calling" Prayers</u>

One of the fascinating memories that I enjoy of my late grandmother, affectionately known as Madea, is that she would rise early in the morning on our farm in Mississippi and call the farm animals to eat. But please understand that this was not just a regular call. This was a call that required the deepest breath from within, and the reservoir of energy from deep inside as a bellowing sound of both command and excitement echoed across the hills of our homestead. Whenever Madea called, those who heard came. The chickens would position themselves near the barriers of the coop, the hogs would scatter recklessly from their pen and the young family members in our home would awaken because we knew breakfast would be prepared soon. Whenever she would call, the animals came and we would arise, because we knew that there was something good waiting for us on the other end of our obedience in coming.

In 2 Corinthians 4:13, Paul says, "We, having the same spirit of faith, according as it is written, I believed and therefore have I spoken; we also believe, and therefore speak." Even in "painful" situations you must be able to speak the Word. Paul is quoting David from Psalm 118:17 when he said, "I shall not die, but live, and declare the works of the Lord."

The prescription works but you've got to keep taking it. You must not look at the things that are seen (or even the things that you are feeling) but you must look at the things which are not seen because the things which are seen are temporal; but the things which are not seen are eternal. (2 Corinthians 4:18) Romans 10:6-8 gives even more clarity and outlines that the righteousness which is of faith is, the Word is near, even in your mouth and in your heart.

The Prescription for Your Pain

You must declare what God has said about you into the atmosphere with your own voice. You must call promises forth that have not yet manifested. For example, you are not denying that sickness exists, but you do deny its right to exist in your body (because of the finished work of Jesus on the cross). Remember, you have been redeemed from the curse of the law and delivered from the authority of darkness. (Galatians 3:13)

You must be willing to call things that are not as though they were until they ARE! Notice too, that you are not calling things that are, as though they are not. You don't deny what exists. You don't deny that sickness exists, but you do deny its right to exist in your body because you have been redeemed from the curse of the law and from the authority of darkness. So, if you don't like what you have, stop saying what you have so that you can have what you say.

Death Sentences

The late Kenneth Hagin Sr. once stated, "People that think wrong believe wrong, and when they believe wrong, they act wrong." The truth of the Word of God needs to invade your thinking, so that you can get all of the wrong out and call all of the right in. Oftentimes, we hinder our prayers and limit God's work in our lives because of the words we speak. We are ensnared by the words that come out of our own mouths. (Proverbs 6:2) We put ourselves in a trap. You may have confined yourself with your own words and now you need to speak words of faith to get out of the trap. Death and life are in the power of your tongue and you will eat from the fruit of what you are speaking. (Proverbs 18:21) Don't give yourself a death sentence!

You must rid yourself of negative confessions like:

1. Money doesn't grow on trees. (It does actually, because money is made from paper which is a byproduct of trees.)
2. I can't afford... (Jesus paid it all.)
3. I am on a fixed income. (Jesus fixed it for you according to John 10:10)
4. I am sick, broke, overwhelmed, etc. (Remember, what was previously stated regarding truth and facts.)

Don't ensnare yourself and hinder your prayers with negative confessions like these. Remember that the earth is voice-activated and your blessings, promises and all that belongs to you is waiting for you to call them in. Practice the principles and watch them work.

SECTION TWO – THE GAME:
Developing the DOERS Strategies for Effective Prayer Initiatives

CHAPTER SEVEN
Hot Stones

"Let seven men of his sons be delivered unto us, and we will hang them up unto the LORD in Gibeah of Saul, whom the LORD did choose. And the king said, I will give them. But the king spared Mephibosheth, the son of Jonathan, the son of Saul, because of the LORD's oath that was between them, between David and Jonathan the son of Saul. But the king took the two sons of Rizpah the daughter of Aiah, whom she bare unto Saul, Armoni and Mephibosheth; and the five sons of Michal the daughter of Saul, whom she brought up for Adriel the son of Barzillai the Meholathite: And he delivered them into the hands of the Gibeonites, and they hanged them in the hill before the LORD: and they fell all seven together, and were put to death in the days of harvest, in the first days, in the beginning of barley harvest. And Rizpah the daughter of Aiah took sackcloth, and spread it for her upon the rock, from the beginning of harvest until water dropped upon them out of heaven, and suffered neither the birds of the air to rest on them by day, nor the beasts of the field by night." 2 Samuel 21:6-10

The story of Rizpah in the bible is a phenomenal rendition of what it means to be a true intercessor. Rizpah was the concubine of the late King Saul. Smith's Bible Dictionary defines concubine as: a wife of second rank where more than one wife was allowed. She was either a Hebrew girl bought; a captive taken in war from the Gentiles; a foreign slave bought or a Canaanite woman, bond or free.

During biblical times, concubines were considered secondary wives. Rizpah's name in Hebrew literally meant a "baking stone" or "hot coal." Oftentimes in the bible, a person's name was indicative of their personality or the characteristics in which their parents foresaw that they would take on. This "fiery" nature of Rizpah compelled her to stand up for her sons. History says that Rizpah guarded the bodies of her sons during the entire barley harvest which lasted from April until October. (Life Application Bible)

She literally stood in the gap, interceded and protected the deceased from the birds of the air during the day time and beasts of the field at night. Rizpah may have been considered second rank, a captive, slave, foreigner or even a foul Canaanite woman but one thing is for certain, she was a true intercessor and warrior! An intercessor is one who stands in the gap for others.

Hot Stones

A true intercessor understands that answered prayers are often the result of perseverance and persistence. It requires the ability to endure obstacles and stay focused on your goals until you overcome. It requires a life of selflessness where you understand the importance of often putting the needs of others before your own so that they can receive breakthrough.

We see this in the life of Rizpah as she protected not only her sons but the bodies of the other slain. Proof that she did this can be found in the fact that when the bodies were finally rescued there were remains left from the others that could be buried as well.

Many believers don't see the fullness of their prayers manifested because they throw in the towel before the race is over. They have not realized that victory in life comes only through staying in the race. You must be willing to press. You must be willing to endure, despite the shame of your situation.

One could only imagine the shame that Rizpah must have encountered having been the king's woman living in high society, eating and drinking the best, and wearing the best. But now her sons were dead and she was in utter despair as they hung on a hill in the capital city, Gibeah of Saul for all to see. What shame and humiliation for her sons to not be buried properly. Surely the people in the region and round about must have mocked her and ridiculed her because of her fall from prominence and the shameful execution of her sons. And to now witness her standing there fending day and night for justice to be brought to their dead flesh could only add more shame. How could any deliverance come from this dead situation?

Like Rizpah, there are many parents, especially mothers, who are fighting daily for their children. They are fighting off the gangs, the drugs, the sexual impurity and the worldly influences. They are fighting off the New Age philosophies, the cultural deception and the anti-Christ spirits. They are fighting for seemingly dead situations to be resurrected. They are fighting for seemingly hopeless situations to receive justice. And like Rizpah, the only way they will prevail in the fight is if they remain hot. Their prayers must remain hot! Their commitment must remain hot! Their conviction must remain hot!

CHAPTER EIGHT
Rizpah's Rock

In order to truly understand the perseverance and the struggle that Rizpah faced, you must journey with me to the time in which she lived. It was a time where there were not any air conditioners or ice makers. This was a time where the heat from the Eastern sun alone was so intense that it could be used to bake bread. To add to this dilemma, some scholars have indicated that Rizpah was of an old age. Yet here she stood in the gap and did not give up until she saw justice on the behalf of her dead sons. There are battles that we will encounter which will require us to fight both day and night. This is why the Lord has given us instructions to meditate on His Word day and night in order for us to be a success. (Joshua 1:8) There are going to be unexpected, unwanted surprises in life that we will have to face. It is during these times that we will either recognize the magnitude of our strength or the disappointment of our weakness.

"If you faint in the day of adversity your strength is small." Proverbs 24:10

Rizpah could have used her energy to murmur, complain and embrace the "woe is me mentality."

After all, the execution of her sons was totally unexpected. Imagine Rizpah enjoying her life of comfort embracing the loving hugs of sons, and then one day waking up to the news of their sudden, brutal, deaths. Her very source of well-being and sustainability was taken from her. In biblical times, it was customary for sons to care for their mothers who were left without a husband to provide for them.

It does not matter if you have a child that is young or old, their untimely death is painful and tragic nonetheless. And only a mother—who has carried that same heartbeat within herself for months, or who has nurtured that child, be it as in infant, an adult or those years in between—only those defined as mother experiences a certain type of painful void that is distinctly different than that of others who suffer the loss. However, Rizpah made a decision that day. She decided that she would stand, fight and persevere until the breakthrough of justice came for her sons.

Build on the Rock

"On Christ, the solid Rock, I stand: All other ground is sinking sand."

Indeed, what an awesome anthem that has been heralded throughout Christendom for many decades. Its lyrics are a constant reminder to believers everywhere of what our faith must be founded upon.

"Therefore whosoever heareth these sayings of mine, and doeth them, I will liken him unto a wise man, which built his house upon a rock: And the rain descended, and the floods came, and the winds blew, and beat upon that house; and it fell not: for it was founded upon a rock." Matthew 7:24-25

Jesus reminds us that wise people are the ones that build their houses upon the rock. Their actions are not built upon the sand which represents that which fades and is temporal and enjoyable only for a season. Sand is found predominately on the shores of beaches. A beach represents a place of fun and relaxation. But when strong rains, hurricanes, typhoons and tsunamis come, the houses built along the beach are the first ones to fall.

Throughout my over twenty years of operating as an intercessor, I have seen many "prayer warriors" and those who call themselves intercessors "fall" as quickly as they rose. Many blew in, blew up and blew out because they had no firm foundation in the Word.

I am reminded of our technological advances and our ability to connect socially over the internet and via telephone. Because of this, more opportunities to spread the message of the Kingdom avail to us as believers. I am particularly fascinated by the many prayer conference calls, internet prayer groups and even Facebook Prayer Pages that are arising. I myself have conducted a daily 5 am prayer ministry since February of 2000. Our prayer group, "POW! WOW! Pray on Warrior! Warrior of Wisdom!" has a motto, "Everyday we Pray!" This prayer ministry was founded during a time that prayer lines and groups in this form were unheard of. As a matter of fact, it might be among the first of its kind. Now, however it is one of many around the nation to the glory of God.

One can appreciate the body of Christ praying more together through such avenues. However, I challenge those who don't have a sincere desire for prayer and those who are not true intercessors. Those who have not examined their motives under the umbrella of purity should be cautioned and careful not to build their houses of prayer on sand. Although I believe that massive groups of believers with pure motives coming together to pray is the Lord's perfect will, ultimately it is always about the effectiveness of the prayers being prayed. Emphasis should never be on the number of people in attendance, but it should be on the power and dimension of breakthrough that is released.

The bible specifically reminds us in relationship to praying that when there are just two or three that are together in prayer God hears and answers. (Matthew 18:19-20)

Years ago I was grieved in my spirit after hearing a mega-church pastor proudly tout of the many hundreds of people that were attending their weeknight prayer call. Although this is an awesome testament of unity being displayed in the body of Christ, when done with selfish motives and ambition it can become detrimental. I caution those that believe that spiritual battles are won based on numbers. In fact, the opposite is the truth. Spiritual battles are based on the effectiveness and fervor (quality) and not the numerics (quantity). (Read the story of Gideon in Judges, Chapters 6–8)

Never forget, vast numbers of believers gathered together in church settings of any kind can certainly warm the heart and even make heaven smile. However, prayer is only recognized by the Father when it is based on pure motives as opposed to popularity or selfish ambition.

Stand on the Rock

Rizpah took her stance of intercession on the rock because she sincerely desired to see the bodies of her dead sons buried. It did not matter that she was considered by some as a second class woman, a harlot or even a cursed woman. Her trust was in Jehovah-Tsidkenu, the Lord God her righteousness, and El Sali, the God who strengthened her, and Jehovah Tsur, God her Rock.

"Behold, the days come, saith the LORD, that I will raise unto David a righteous Branch, and a King shall reign and prosper, and shall execute judgment and justice in the earth. In his days, Judah shall be saved, and Israel shall dwell safely: and this is his name whereby he shall be called, THE LORD OUR RIGHTEOUSNESS." Jeremiah 23:5-6

"I will say unto God my rock, Why hast thou forgotten me? Why go I mourning because of the oppression of the enemy?" Psalm 42:9

El Sali (God of my strength) is referenced here in Psalm 42.

Jehovah Tsur (Rock) is referenced five times in the "Song" of Moses: (Deuteronomy 32:4, 15, 18, 30-31)

The dead bodies of our slain sons and daughters are crying out for God's people to take a stance on the Rock. It will not be the prayers of community leaders, famous singers, admired athletes, wealthy businessmen, popular entertainers or political officials that will put a stop to the violence in our streets, but it will be the persistent, persevering prayers of the "Rock Standers" that will bring breakthrough and deliverance to our world.

"If my people, which are called by my name, shall humble themselves, and pray, and seek my face, and turn from their wicked ways; then will I hear from heaven, and will forgive their sin, and will heal their land." (2 Chronicles 7:14)

The Sackcloth of the Suffering

Not only can a rock be a hard place, but the bible says Rizpah based her intercession from a place that was not pleasant. Sackcloth represented sorrow, grief and mourning. When worn, this cloth publicly announced that the wearer had a broken heart and a sorrowful spirit. (Wilson's Dictionary of Bible Types) It also represents the public expression of humiliation and penitence in view of some misfortune, present or impending. (biblegateway.com)

Although many translations of 2 Samuel 21:10 interpret Rizpah's sackcloth as her laying on it, upon further examination you will find that instead of her spreading it upon the rock she spread it **against the rock**, so as to form a little hut or shelter to protect her from the glaring blaze of the sunshine. The word "upon" has led many commentators to suppose that she used it as a bed; but this is not the meaning of the Hebrew. (biblehub.com)

True intercession will often come as a result of being placed in a "hard" place. It was after the death of my brother and sister-in-law (as referenced in the Introduction) that my prayer life went to another dimension. There was good reason for this in that their three smallest children were left orphaned, and my husband and I took them in. Prior to this tragedy, my husband and I did not desire neither did we feel we had any time in our lives to be responsible for raising more children. However, now we found ourselves in a hard place, a rough place. There were several scenarios the children were facing. They could be raised by another relative that did not have a mind to care for them; be raised by one that desired to take them in but could not provide them with the best upbringing, or foster care (which we never would have allowed).

After first praying, and then talking to each other, we felt that our home and our parenting would be what was best for these children. Having made that decision, I wish I could tell you that a happily ever after scenario came next. Instead, we have endured a season of roughness. From custody battles to exaggerated, unethical legal fees, the path has been rough. It has seemed as though we woke up one morning and were fighting someone else's battle. For a season, there were seven of us cramped into one 1,800 square foot home, already occupied by a family plus two business offices that took up a significant amount of space. There were new responsibilities, new challenges, new personalities, new behavioral issues and new financial woes with more mouths to feed and limited income. There was harsh treatment by family, and negative words spoken. It was rough but we were determined to stick with it and stand on our Rock. In the midst of it all, we have emerged more mature and determined than ever. El Sali stepped in and strengthened us. Jehovah Tsur kept us standing, and in due season we were blessed with another home almost three times the size of the one we had.

We persevered and were persistent in prayer and faith. We did not stop praying and believing God's Hand to move until we saw the rain come. Years later the children are adjusting. We call them the Jream Team after the youngest, whose name is Jream meaning "Jesus Rules Everything Around Me." Like arrows in our hands, our prayers are helping us to direct them so that they can be released into a bright future, bringing deliverance to many. (Psalms 127:4)

Like Rizpah, we were in unexpected warfare after sudden deaths, but we learned how to stand on the Rock!

CHAPTER NINE
Until Heavy Rain Falls

Imagine having to consume the stench of seven naked, decomposing bodies that have been baking under the hot, scorching Eastern sun. Above, at a distance, circling anxiously are the shadows of vultures whose greatest desire is to tear into the dead carcasses of your loved ones. Vultures are the nasty, vile scavengers that gorge on their prey. After consumption they eventually fall into a sleep like stupor.

These vultures are like the people that gossip and publicly share your secret struggles and shameful situations. They are so intense and engaged that when they are finally done all their energy has been exhausted, having expended it all on minding your business.

These foul creatures were a constant daily threat against the flesh of the deceased. Warding them off became the constant daily life struggle that Rizpah endured from sun up to sun down. But then by night, she was faced with an even greater challenge as the beasts of the fields howled and hissed with hunger for the flesh of her boys. I imagine that being like the gangsters that roam the city streets of my home Chicago. These vultures thirst for the blood of the young and even innocent. They seek to kill and they seek to destroy those that do not join their gang affiliations and violent, criminal initiatives. More often than not, the young and the innocent give in only to keep from being taken out. Although, some have mothers like Rizpah who will stop at nothing to preserve their dignity, others do not. So, their predators continue to prevail, wreaking havoc in the night and terror in the day.

The threatening sounds and unimaginable terror of the night coupled with the unknown that darkness often brings certainly must have left Rizpah wondering if her intercession was worth it. The silhouettes of creatures that traveled in packs now lurking nearby strategizing their ambush surely must have caused her to have second thoughts regarding her night watch, yet she did not give up, instead she prevailed.

One commentator painted it like this:

Those seven dead bodies remained exposed for six months, as a grim trophy of Gibeonite vengeance. Until water dropped upon them out of heaven; Hebrew, **was poured upon them**; until copious and heavy rains came. The outpouring of these rains would put an end to the famine, and be regarded as a proof that the wrath of Heaven was appeased. There is no reason for supposing that these rains came before the usual period, in autumn, which was about the middle of October. Thus, for six months, with no other protection than her mantle of sackcloth hung against the rock, this noble woman watched the decaying bodies of her loved ones, until at last her devoted conduct touched David's heart, and their remains were honorably interred. (www.biblehub.com)

You can't stop praying until the rain comes. You may feel dry, parched, withered and even burnt out, but don't stop because the rain is coming.

Overcoming Burn Out

"Now there is at Jerusalem by the sheep market, a pool, which is called in the Hebrew tongue Bethesda, having five porches. In these lay a great multitude of impotent folk, of blind, lame, withered, waiting for the moving of the water. For an angel went down at a certain season into the pool, and troubled the water: whosoever then first after the troubling of the water stepped in was made whole of whatsoever disease he had." John 5:2-4

Not only were the people that hung out at this pool impotent (powerless), blind, halt (stuck), but they were withered. The word here for withered is the Greek word *xeros* which means dry. These were people that had been scorched. Life had burnt them. Circumstances had burnt them. It literally meant that they were deprived of their natural juices, shrunk, wasted and withered. Their motivation and natural inspiration from within had waned. They needed to be refreshed. They needed to experience the rain.

Deuteronomy 28:12 says: "The LORD shall open unto thee His good treasure, the heaven to give the rain unto thy land in his season, and to bless all the work of thine hand: and thou shalt lend unto many nations, and thou shalt not borrow."

<u>Seasons of Breakthrough</u>

Most of our blessings and breakthrough will come as we practice the principles found in the Word of GOD. However, some only will come as a result of our due season.

Notice in John, Chapter 5 that it was during a certain season that the angels troubled the water.

Don't miss your *kairos* moment! *Kairos* is the Greek word for opportune time. There are open windows and portals in the spirit realm where there is more opportunity to access the blessings of God.

Things You Should Know About Seasons, Timings & Special Days

- Special things happen on special days.

Acts 2:1 – "And when the day of Pentecost was fully come, they were all with one accord in one place."

- There is an appointed time for everything.

Ecclesiastes 3:1 – "To everything there is a season, and a time to every purpose under the heaven:"

- There is a DUE SEASON assigned to everything.

Leviticus 26:4 – "Then I will give you rain in due season, and the land shall yield her increase, and the trees of the field shall yield their fruit".

- Seasons are appointed times.

Numbers 9:2 – "Let the children of Israel also keep the Passover at his appointed season."

- Birth to spiritual and natural things takes place during certain seasons. You have an appointed season for your breakthrough.

2 Kings 4:17 – "And the woman conceived, and bore a son at that season that Elisha had said unto her, according to the time of life."

- Your prosperity has been designated to fully manifest in a certain season.

Psalm 1:3 – "And he shall be like a tree planted by the rivers of water, that bringeth forth his fruit in his season; his leaf also shall not wither; and whatsoever he doeth shall prosper."

- There is a season appointed to speak certain things.

Proverbs 15:23 – "A man hath joy by the answer of his mouth: and a word spoken in due season, how good is it!"

- There is a former and latter rain that comes in season.

Jeremiah 5:24 – "Neither say they in their heart, Let us now fear the LORD our God, that giveth rain, both the former and the latter, in his season: he reserveth unto us the appointed weeks of the harvest."

- Prophetic manifestation has a season.

Luke 1:20 – "And, behold, thou shalt be dumb, and not able to speak, until the day that these things shall be performed, because thou believest not my words, which shall be fulfilled in their season."

- Temptation comes for a season.

Luke 4:13 – "And when the devil had ended all the temptation, he departed from him for a season."

- Times and seasons belong to God.

Acts 1:8 – "But ye shall receive power, after that the Holy Ghost is come upon you: and ye shall be witnesses unto me both in Jerusalem, and in all

Judaea, and in Samaria, and unto the uttermost part of the earth."

- Reaping comes in due season.

Galatians 6:9 – "And let us not be weary in well doing: for in due season we shall reap, if we faint not."

Rizpah stood on her rock and under her sackcloth of shelter until the season of the heavy rains came. It was not until that season manifested that justice prevailed for her. It was not until that season that King David, so ashamed of this oversight, ordered the proper burial due to all of the deceased. Her answered prayer did not happen before the rain came or after it had subsided. It did not come because she was popular or pretty, a harlot or a holy woman. It did not come because she was tired and weary. It came because it was time for the season of rain and because of her persistency, perseverance and determination to wait until her prayer was answered and the dignity of the deceased's memory preserved.

You must embrace the fact that sometimes your blessings and breakthroughs are appointed to a certain season. In the meantime, you must be persistent and persevere in prayer until the manifestation comes.

I hear the sound of an abundance of rain. (1 Kings 18:41) So, get ready, it's on the way!

CHAPTER TEN
Failure Is Only Feedback

In Romans 8:36-37 we are reminded that no matter what we go through and encounter in life, we have complete victory through Jesus Christ. There is no failure when you are in Christ! Failure to the believer simply means there is room to grow, learn, change and trust God even more. You must not so much try to avoid failure as you must focus on training yourself to succeed.

The Lord is calling you to maturity (Ephesians 4:13) so that your prayers can be more effective. Maturity and change comes with training yourself. Notice they don't just come as a result of trying. For instance, you will never win a 5K race by just trying, you actually have to train. You must be willing to exercise yourself towards godliness. (1 Timothy 4:7)

You train yourself by:

1. Recognizing where you may have missed it instead of just blaming the outcome of the situation on something outside of your ability.
2. Repenting for "missing it" either knowingly or unknowingly. When you repent, you now have a new perspective on the situation. You now see where you have sinned which is a

literal meaning for missing the mark and it also means to:

Wander from the Word of God.

3. Being accountable to the Word of God and what it says you should do concerning your situation.
4. Practicing the disciplines that will help foster your spiritual growth: effective prayer, study of the Word, attending church, keeping good company, etc.
5. Developing a relationship with the Holy Spirit and learning to listen and discern His voice.

You are now positioning yourself as a true believer because you are "being" who God has called you to be and "leaving" the old person behind. You don't be-stay (stay the way you are), you be-lieve (leave where you are) and excel higher in life.

Seek to Know

In 1 Kings 3, because Solomon asked for wisdom on how to walk out his purpose, God gave him wealth. Wisdom often proceeds your blessings and breakthroughs in life. There is a revealing that takes place. A light comes in and dispels the darkness that has been over your situation. You are receiving

Failure Is Only Feedback

feedback from your dilemma. You can now learn and grow.

Acts 2:20 references the day of the Lord as being great and notable. The Word notable here comes from the Greek word *epiphanes* meaning conspicuous, manifest and illustrious. This word is also in relationship to the phrase "to give light" in Luke 1:79 where the scripture tells us that Jesus (the Dayspring) came to give light to those who were in darkness. The word is *epiphaino* which means to shine upon, i.e. become (literally) visible or (figuratively) known: appear, give light. Thayer's Greek Lexicon defines it:

1. to show to or upon:
2. to bring to light
3. to appear, become visible
4. of stars
5. to become clearly known, to show one's self

The Lord wants our situations to be made clearly known to us. Thus feedback comes through either wisdom taught to us by man or given to us by God, or by experiencing personal failure. Have you ever heard the expression, "God never wastes a hurt?"

In Genesis 50:20, after being sold in slavery by his brothers, estranged from his loving father for decades and imprisoned in a foreign land for years, Joseph was able to examine his situation and wisely declare that what his brothers meant for evil, God meant for good, in order to save many people!

When you are able to properly assess the failures in your life, you can understand First Thessalonians 5:18, which reminds us that in everything we are to give thanks because it is God's will for us to do so. And Romans 8:28 further reminds us that all things work together for good to them that love God, and to them who are called according to His purpose.

You must no longer allow Satan, the god of this world (2 Corinthians 4:4), to blind you and keep you from seeing, understanding and knowing what is going on in your life and hindering you in the spirit realm from getting breakthrough in prayer. Deuteronomy 29:4 references a perceiving heart as a mind that understands, eyes that see and ears that

Failure Is Only Feedback

hear. The word perceive here is *yada* which means to know. It also means:

1. to perceive and see
2. learn to know
3. find out and discern
4. to know by experience
5. to recognize, admit, acknowledge, confess
6. to consider
7. be acquainted with
8. to know how, be skillful in
9. to have knowledge, be wise

You must perceive the feedback your situation is providing you. The Lord is bringing light to you in that failed circumstance so you can understand both how to clearly pray and how to properly conduct yourself concerning it. When you are able to take the feedback from the failure, you can use it to fight. You will never know how to properly engage in spiritual warfare if you do not gain the necessary wisdom. Remember, the wisdom will either come through instruction or experience. Oftentimes, believers fail to pay attention to their previous failed experiences either because of the shame or the pain. Don't allow this to be your hindrance.

CHAPTER ELEVEN
Turning Tragedy into Triumph

Rizpah's sons were executed. They died prematurely and were taken from the earth before their time. There was only one thing she could do. After all, the only thing left remaining for a mother to do after having a child die prematurely is to preserve the dignity of their memory. So, Rizpah positioned herself in warfare and for almost half a year she fought to keep her children from being devoured. She had to roll up her sleeves and get to the work of interceding. There was a messy situation on her hands and she had to get downright dirty to receive the results she was looking for.

Building Altars

On that rock of Gibeah (meaning hill) she stationed herself and her intercession. Notice that she did not station herself at the courts of an earthly king to request mercy and justice for her deceased sons. Instead she built an altar of sacrifice amidst relentless opposition that she had to fight against day and night. Prayers that get results will require that we build altars.

1. Building altars symbolizes commitment to getting what you are petitioning for.
2. Building altars represents the place where you have a personal encounter with the Lord. (Abram built one in Sichem, a place where God met him. Genesis 12)

3. Building altars makes provision for refuge in the midst of conflict and battle. (Jacob built one after departing from his home due to conflict with his brother Esau.)
4. Building altars requires faith. (When the Lord showed Abram the land of Canaan and promised him that He would give it to him, the land was filled with Canaanites who were the most perverted and corrupt culture in human history. During Abram's time they were like the modern day Satanists. Yet Abram built an altar anyway as a symbol of His acceptance of God's promise, despite the negative circumstances.)
5. Building altars requires sacrifice. Altars represent a place of meeting God. Whenever you meet God, some form of worship is always required. True worship is always a sacrifice. It's a sacrifice to worship the Lord when your situation is dictating tragedy as opposed to triumph. You are still to offer a sacrifice of praise unto God. (Hebrews 13:15)
6. Building altars creates possibilities as we intercede, standing before God and petitioning Him to intervene in our earthly affairs. (We give Him room to move.)
7. Building altars creates memorials to remember the victories we have won as a result of our prayer perseverance.

Turning Tragedy into Triumph

<u>Digging Wells</u>

Not only must we understand the role of building altars in relationship to prayer results, but we must also understand the significance of digging wells. Building altars requires making sacrifices. Digging wells require us to stretch ourselves so that we can go deep.

In Genesis Chapter 26, we find the story of Isaac going back to a place where his father Abraham had dug a well. He began to dig the well again because the Philistines had stopped it up. The bible says that the people of the land argued that the well belonged to them, so Isaac named the well Esek which means *contention* or *quarrelling*. Isaac moved from there and dug another well and the people likewise opposed him concerning that well so he named it Sitna which meant *strife* or *accusations*. The next place Isaac went to and dug a well, he did not encounter opposition so he named it Rehoboth which meant *God has made room*.

This biblical account of Isaac digging wells illustrates how opposing forces come to "stop up" and try to take away our blessings. There are at least three dimensions of opposition that you have to breakthrough in order to get your prayers answered and reach your place of refreshing. The first dimension is in the area of contention. This is because negotiations are happening in the spirit realm as Satanic forces are contending with the angelic beings that have been assigned to bring your breakthrough. There is a quarrel going on. A struggle has ensued and you must earnestly contend to maintain your faith so that your heavenly helpers can bring about your breakthrough. (Jude 1:3)

The next dimension is in the area of accusations. Revelations 12:10 says that Satan is accusing believers day and night. Likewise, Rizpah had the fowl of the air to contend with during the day and the beast of the field to fight against at night.

In Job, Chapter 1, we witness an account of Satan himself reporting before the throne of God after lurking throughout all the earth examining the activity of mankind. The Message Translation calls Satan the Designated Accuser. This is important to note and one of the main reasons why it is so essential to keep a heart of repentance. While praying for your breakthrough, you don't want anything to show up on your record that Satan can use against you to keep you from getting your answers. This is why Mark 11:25-26 emphasizes the importance of forgiving, which is to let go of the transgressions others have committed against you. If you hold on to them, Satan has room to accuse you.

Not only did the Lord make room for Isaac at Rehoboth after he persevered through the contention and accusation, but Isaac was able to prophesy that he would be fruitful in that place. That night the Lord visited him and sealed the prophetic word he had spoken by declaring a blessing over him. The next account of what happens is very interesting because we see Isaac's enemies coming to him to make a treaty. There was so much favor and blessing on Isaac's life that they had to acknowledge God was with him. As a result, they did not want to strive against him. When Isaac forgave them and accepted their treaty, Isaac's servants reported that they found water in a well they had been digging. He had reached a place of triumph!

Isaac named that well Sheba or Beersheba which meant place of oath. I believe that Isaac would not have been able to continuously prosper had he not forgiven his enemies. Total forgiveness and being free of all sin, both your sin and the sin of others, is the final dimension of total prayer breakthrough. This is a realm where your conscience is totally free of issues, accusations, and ought (natural expectations). It's a dimension in maturity that you have reached because there is an understanding of where your fight is at and who it is truly with.

Our Fight

"Finally, my brethren, be strong in the Lord, and in the power of his might. Put on the whole armour of God, that ye may be able to stand against the wiles of the devil. For we wrestle not against flesh and blood, but against principalities, against powers, against the rulers of the darkness of this world, against spiritual wickedness in high places." Ephesians 6:10-12

Knowing who your fight is against is one challenge. Knowing how to fight is yet another. You must know how to stand against the wiles of the devil. This simply means knowing his methods which is from the Greek word *methodia*: to follow-up by method and settled plan, using deceit, craft and trickery. (Thayer's Greek Lexicon)

The enemy has a follow-up plan on you. He knows your history and your family's history and comes to follow-up on every door, window and crack in your life that is vulnerable. He is looking for that crack in your conscience that is holding on to the transgressions of others, even if it is just a little bit of resentment; even if there is just a tiny sting of negative remembrance.

When Satan visited God in heaven he had been scouting Job out. He had been considering him. Job was a great man full of integrity and he honored God.

However, there was a crack in his armor for Satan to come in, because of fear in his life. The bible indicates that Job literally said out of his mouth, "The thing I have greatly feared has come upon me. (Job 3:25) We can even see Job in great concern regarding the actions of his children, so much so until every time they threw a party he would make offerings to amend for any potential sins that they had committed.

Offerings are to always be given in faith and not out of worry, fear or concern. As a matter of fact, anything that we do outside of faith is considered sin. (Romans 14:23) Additionally, it is impossible to please God without doing what we do in faith. (Hebrews 11:6)

The enemy had access to test Job in the area of His trusting God because he had feared. This is why God allowed the enemy to consider Job. The enemy is considering how he can get a stronghold in your life. This is why the bible says we are to give no place to the devil. (Ephesians 4:27) The NIV translation of this verse states: "And do not give the devil a foothold."

You must not give the devil opportunity and room to get into your life. You must be so tight with God that there is no place for the devil to fit. So when injustice shows up in your life, you have all of heaven's resources and backing to stand against it and triumph!

Standing Against Injustice

The way to stand against injustice is to stand in truth. You stand in truth when you stand on the Word of God. In her book, *Spiritual Housekeeping – Sweep Your Life Free from Demonic Strongholds and Satanic Oppression,* Apostle Kimberly Daniels highlights how the spirit of injustice known as Cockatrice works:

> I have studied the cockatrice spirit for many years. My interest was raised when I found that Isaiah uses it as a spiritual analogy. Apparently, this mythological creature was important enough for Isaiah to use to make his point. It is said to have a head, legs, and wings like a cock, but a body and tail like a serpent. The danger of the creature is that it was said to have the power to kill a person who looked into its eyes, with one glance. I believe that this is a spirit that needs to be dealt with when we are under legal attack…

Apostle Daniels continues:

> These are the manifestations of an antichrist system that is rooted in secular humanism. The mind-binding spirit that under-girds this demonic attack is the strongman called **Cockatrice**. As men look into the eyes of this demon, they cannot see truth, right is perverted, and wrong is celebrated.
>
> Even in corrupt systems of the world, the righteous prevail. The High Court of Heaven trumps the Supreme Court of the land. The Lord has positioned godly people throughout the systems of the world to fight for the things of His Kingdom. The abominations of courts, corrections, probation, parole, and law enforcement do not go unnoticed. The Lord sees it all. According to their deeds they will pay. In the meantime, we must be laborers (with God) to stand in the gap against the injustices of the world. Legal and political oppression is under our feet, but we must stand to put spiritual pressure on the powers that be, so that we can experience justice in our homes and in the streets of our cities.

Adapted from:
http://www.hiskingdomprophecy.com/the-cockatrice-the-spirit-of-injustice/)

To get more revelation on this scripture as it relates to the spirit of injustice, read Isaiah Chapter 59 in the Amplified Version of the bible.

Triumph After Tragedy

When tragedy occurs it often happens in a moment's notice. However, it is the suffering that always seems to last a life time. During the suffering, there is a battle taking place, not only in the heavenlies but in the minds of men. Anyone who has ever suffered a tragedy knows too well the distress that accompanies it. The days turn into weeks, which turns into months and before you know it, years later you find yourself still trying to pick up the pieces from that one tragic event.

It has been over seven years since Reggie & Charnell's deaths, yet our family is still adjusting to some of those initial challenges we were presented with. Although we are not just surviving but thriving today, to say that it has been challenging would be an understatement of great magnitude. The good news is that I can report of situation after situation, with testimony of how the miraculous has intervened in our lives to keep us going. However, the greatest testimony I can give is that it is because of the prayers of the righteous that we have come this far.

Turning Tragedy into Triumph

When I think of Rizpah, I wonder if she actually witnessed the execution of her sons on that tragic day in late April, early May. I wonder if like some of the parents today whose children have succumbed to a similar fate, after the debris has been removed from the busy city street and the police tape has been taken down, is that when she arrived, only to hear of what had happened and not to witness it with her own eyes, which I'm sure would have been worse.

Scripture does not tell us those details. Nevertheless, the one and most important thing that we know is that she guarded their bodies while they hung, hopeless on that hill. From the beginning of harvest season around April until "water dropped upon them out of heaven" sometime in October, Rizpah interceded.

She did not give up because she knew that the rain would eventually come. And with the rain would come her results; her answered prayer. Whenever intercession goes up, heaven must come down. When heaven comes to the earth it gets the attention of the kings in the earth. King David heard about what Rizpah had done and he set in motion the proper burial for Saul and all of his sons.

The Amplified Bible of 2 Samuel 21:14 says:

"...After that, God was moved by prayer for the land."

There is a discrepancy among bible theologians as to whether the rain came as a result of the sons being executed to amend the injustice done against the Gibeonites, or after their bodies were buried to amend for Saul and his sons not being given the proper burial and honor due a king and his sons. The details of these facts are up for argument, but one thing we know for sure is that God was moved by prayer for the land, the rain came and Rizpah triumphed in her intercession!

# SECTION THREE – THE GO: Doing It! Going from Information & Impartation to Application & Activation

CHAPTER TWELVE
Prayers that Get Results

<u>Kingly Authority Activation</u>

(Keep in mind that with this prayer, you are praying from a high place looking down and decreeing, declaring and dictating what needs to take place in your sphere of influence. Think of a king seated on his throne. His throne is always elevated above everyone and everything else in his presence. Now think of looking down on the earth from an airplane. Your problems look smaller and you feel bigger. This is the mindset you need to have and the position in which you need to pray from when you are operating in your kingly authority.)

Father in the Name of Jesus, I come to you having examined myself with Your Word and repented of all hindrances and occurrences where I have missed the mark, fallen short of Your glory and wandered from your Word. I renounce all spirits of condemnation, guilt, shame and worthlessness that would try to sear my conscience and remind me of past sins, wrongs, or hurts committed by others toward me or me towards others.

Your Word says I can ascend to Your holy hill only with a pure heart and clean hands. Therefore, I renounce impure thoughts, motives and words that have been spoken by me and against others. May the blood of Jesus wash my conscience clean of dead works now. May His completed work on the cross free me from all past negativity.

Father, may Jesus' intercession as He is seated on the throne at Your Right Hand now give me access to my place and seat in heaven. I walk in my authority as a king. I decree and I declare all of heaven's resources are at my disposal to advance God's Kingdom in the earth. I advance it now through my prayers. My prayers are efficient and effective and they accomplish much.

The angels of the Lord are near and they hear the will of God as I voice prayers founded from the Word of God. They are ready to take flight. The angels assigned to my life are ready to excel in strength and accomplish their tasks. They are listening and they are moving. They are servicing me, an heir of salvation, now in Jesus' Name!

(Scripture References: John 17:17, Romans 3:23, 1 Timothy 4:2, Psalm 24:2-4, Hebrews 9:14, John 19:30, Romans 8:34, Ephesians 2:6, Revelation 5:10, Ephesians 1:3, 2 Peter 1:3, Matthew 11:12, James 5:16, Psalm 103:20, Hebrews 1:14)

Prayers that Get Results

Priestly Position Activation

(Remember from this prayer position you are boldly – because Jesus gives you access - yet humbly – because you are making a petition - approaching the throne of God to present petitions on behalf of yourself and others. It's like you are praying from a place here on earth looking up to God asking Him to intervene in the affairs of mankind down here. It is like a child kneeling at bedtime and asking God for protection as they sleep.)

Father in the Name of Jesus I come to You now having asked for forgiveness for all of my sins committed against Your Word and others. I ask that You would create in me a clean heart and renew in me a right spirit so that I may properly intercede on behalf of others. Your Word has said that men are to always pray and not faint.

Therefore, I gird up my loins with the truth of the Word and prepare myself to bear down, so that I may push through and bring forth breakthrough in the land as a result of my availing prayers.

I am called by Your Name so I humble my heart to seek Your face. I turn away from anything and everything that would keep me from trusting You. You are the solution to the problems in our land. Send forth Your Mighty Hand of deliverance to the earth. Have mercy on your people. Hide not your face from us. Hear our cry Oh Lord and attend unto our prayer!

(Scripture References: 1 John 1:9, Psalm 51:10, Luke 18:1, Ephesians 6:14, Jeremiah 17:11a, Psalm 27:8, Isaiah 65:1, Romans 9:18, Psalm 27:9, Psalm 61:1)

Prayers for Children

Lord, Your Word says that children are a heritage from You and a reward to parents. May my children bring forth happiness and not sorrow. May they be the head and not the tail. May they be above the circumstances in life and not underneath them. May they be blessed in the city and blessed in the field. May the works my children produce be blessed and honorable to You. May they be blessed when they travel and wherever they go. May their enemies fall and be defeated. When they come at them one way may they flee seven ways.

May the anointing of the three Hebrew boys Shadrach (real name Hananiah), Meshach (real name Mishael) and Abednego (real name Azariah) be upon my children. May they excel even in the midst of a foreign people in a foreign land. May they have godly alliances and peers; people who will stand with them against evil and perversion. May they be ten times greater than their worldly counterparts. May the anointing of Daniel rest upon them:

> The anointing of wisdom, discretion, prudence and honor.
>
> The anointing of purity, steadfastness, and commitment.
>
> The anointing of eloquence, excellence and greatness.
>
> The anointing of royalty, majesty and courage.
>
> The anointing to dream, see and discern.
>
> The anointing to clearly think, articulate excellently in speech and influence the masses.

May the anointing of David rest upon my children. At a young age David served you and had a heart to please you. He walked circumspective, humbly and selflessly tending your sheep. He did not seek after fame, fortune or recognition. Yet you exalted Him Lord. Like David, may my children be promoted in their season and not before Your time. You are the God that makes all things beautiful in Your time. May my children have the anointing to wait on You. Like David:

> May they tend to Your will and seek after Your way.

> May they learn to wait on You when their strength seems to wane.
>
> May they have boldness to speak against the enemy who tries to defy.
>
> May they have trust enough in You to fight against the giants in their lives.
>
> May they have humility enough to repent when they have done wrong.
>
> May they have hope enough to know that You will never forsake them no matter how challenging their lives may become.

Lord, as Your angel visited Mary, may my children experience supernatural visitations from You. May they receive the direction they need to fulfill their purpose in life. Like Mary:

> May they desire to live a pure and holy life before You.
>
> May they trust in You with all of their heart and not lean unto their own understanding.
>
> May they honor righteous living and holiness for without it no man can see You.

May they obey You despite the opposition, shame, humiliation, ridicule or guilt that might come with their decision.

May they be full of grace.

May they put Your plans before their plans.

May they hear and discern Your leading.

May they walk in the supernatural and experience miracles throughout their lives.

May they always remember that You are Abba, their source and their supply.

May they never be as orphans in the land.

When those that should nurture them, mother them and father them forsake them, Lord You lift them up. When all the people of the earth turn against them, Lord You don't forsake them. When life knocks them down, You pick them up.

My children are Yours. They belong to You. Help me to raise them to revere You and submit to Your admonition. Like Jesus, may they grow in wisdom and in stature and receive Your favor as well as the favor of man.

May they have hearts of compassion to save their world.

May they be givers and not just receivers.

May they be disciplined and orderly.

May they cast off rebellion, disobedience and stubbornness.

May they be quick to hear and slow to speak.

May they desire to please their parents but most of all You, their Father.

May they understand their purpose at a young age and walk boldly in it.

May they be saved from the seduction, perversion and deception of their generation.

May they influence their culture and their culture not influence them.

May they take care of and honor their parents that they may have a long life on the earth.

May it go well with them in school, business, on their jobs, in their careers, marriages, relationships and with their finances.

May they not walk in the counsel of the ungodly and stand among those who practice sin.

May they have the discipline to step away from those who ridicule Your Word.

May they fight the good fight of faith and always come out a winner.

May they finish their course well.

At an old age, when they are ready to sleep and step off into eternity to be in Your Presence, may they be able to say as David said, "I was young and now I am old yet I have never seen the righteous forsaken, nor his seed begging for bread!"

(Scripture References: Psalm 127:1-3, Deuteronomy 28, The Book of Daniel, 1 Samuel 16-17, Luke 1, Psalm 25:7, Psalm 27:10, Luke 2:52, John 3:16, Matthew 3:17, Ephesians 6:2-3, Exodus 20:12, Psalm 1, Psalm 27, 1 Timothy 6:12, Psalm 37:25)

Prayers Against Premature Death

"Do not be overwicked, and do not be a fool - why die before your time?" (Ecclesiastes 7:17 NIV)

In the Name of Jesus, I come against untimely and premature death! Lord, I thank You that I live a long life pleasing to You. I desire to walk worthy before You, being fruitful in every good work and increasing in Your knowledge. I desire to keep Your commandments, and do those things that are pleasing in Your sight.

I declare that I will think good thoughts. I will think on things that are true, honest, just, pure, lovely, of a good report, that have virtue and are praise-worthy.

I will do good deeds and I will only let excellent communication proceed out of my mouth. I present my body to You as a living sacrifice. I do that which is pure and holy with my body. I receive good health in my body and my mind. I am in good health and I prosper even as my soul prospers. Therefore, I receive the promise of 120 years of life on earth with the full functioning of my mind and the faculties of my body.

My soul is redeemed from the power of the grave. Every covenant of death assigned to my life is null and void. I am not in agreement with any plans from hell over my life. I will not be trampled by the enemy.

Lord, I pray that You satisfy me and my family with long life and show us Your salvation. Take away from among us, the spirit of untimely death. I resist and repel anything or situation that can cause untimely death in me or my family.

I will not die when I am young or middle-aged. I will not see the grave until I am a ripe old age! No weapon that has been formed against me can prosper. Every tongue that rises against me in judgment is condemned. I declare I am the redeemed of the Lord and I have been saved from the curse of death, hell and the grave!

Prayers that Get Results

(Scripture References: Nehemiah 13:14, Philippians 4:8, Colossians 1:10, I John 3:22, Genesis 6:3, Psalm 49:15, Isaiah 28:18, Psalm 102:24, Job 5:26, Isaiah 54:17, Psalm 107:2, 1 Corinthians 15:55, Psalm 91:6, Revelation 1:18)

<u>Prayers for Endurance</u>

I will endure until the end and be saved! (Matthew 24:13)

Lord, I will trust in and be rooted in Your Word. When affliction and persecution comes I will not be offended. (Mark 4:17)

Lord, may my love help me to endure all things. (1 Corinthians 13:7)

I am patient and my faith endures through persecutions and tribulations. (2 Thessalonians 1:4)

I will endure hardness, as a good soldier of Jesus Christ. (2 Timothy 2:3)

I patiently endure so that I can obtain my promise. (Hebrews 6:15)

All of heaven is cheering me on, therefore I will lay aside every weight and besetting sins and I will run this race that is set before me with patience. (Hebrews 12:1)

Like Jesus, the author and finisher of my faith, I will get a picture of the joy of overcoming this. I will endure this cross and I will ignore this shame because I too am seated in heavenly places with Christ Jesus. (Hebrews 12:2)

I will endure this opposition and I will not be weary and faint in my mind. (Hebrews 12:3)

I will endure this chastening because it is my Father. He loves me and knows what is best for me. (Hebrews 12:7)

I love the Lord, therefore I am blessed and I am able to endure temptation. When it is all over I will receive the crown of life that has been promised to me! (James 1:12)

May I be blessed with the patience of Job to endure and find happiness in this situation. (James 5:11)

Lord, help me to pace myself so that I can finish my race for I understand that the winner is not the swift one and the battle is not won by the strong. Help me to not give up. (Ecclesiastes 9:11a)

"I press toward the mark for the prize of the high calling of God in Christ Jesus." (Philippians 3:14)

Lord, help me to be an intercessor for my family, nation and the world. (Isaiah 59:16)

Prayers that Get Results

Like Jesus, Lord help me to continuously intercede for others. (Hebrews 7:25)

I declare that I will always pray and not faint. (Luke 18:1)

I do pray without ceasing. (1 Thessalonians 5:17)

Lord, may my prayers set captives free. (Acts 12:5)

I will not cease to make mention of others in my prayers night and day. (Romans 1:9 & 2 Timothy 1:3)

Lord, I thank You that when I call You, You answer and You show me great and mighty things that I did not know. (Jeremiah 33:3)

I am not afraid of the terror in the night or the arrows that fly in the day. (Psalm 91:5)

Lord, may Your judgment and justice prevail in this situation! (Job 8:3)

May the poor and fatherless be defended! May justice come to the afflicted and to the needy. (Psalm 82:3)

Lord, I have done judgment and justice: leave me not to my oppressors. (Psalm 119:121)

May the judgement and justice of the Lord be executed over my situation. (Jeremiah 23:5)

I will not faint, fear, tremble or be terrified because of my enemies. (Deuteronomy 20:3)

I will not faint for I will see the goodness of the Lord in the land of the living. (Psalm 27:13)

My strength is great, therefore I will not faint in the day of adversity! (Proverbs 24:10)

I receive God's power and strength therefore I will not faint. (Isaiah 40:29)

I will wait in the presence of the Lord. Therefore, my strength is renewed. I mount up and soar like an eagle. I run and I am not weary. I will walk and not faint. (Isaiah 40:31)

Lord, I receive Your mercy and I will not faint. I am renewed day by day and I will not faint. (2 Corinthians 4:1)

Prayer Against Evil

Psalm 140
For the director of music. A psalm of David.

Rescue me, LORD, from evildoers; protect me from the violent, who devise evil plans in their hearts and stir up war every day. They make their tongues as sharp as a serpent's; the poison of vipers is on their lips. Keep me safe, LORD, from the hands of the wicked; protect me from the violent, who devise ways to trip my feet. The arrogant have hidden a snare for me; they have spread out the cords of their net and have set traps for me along my path. I say to the LORD, "You are my God." Hear, LORD, my cry for mercy. Sovereign LORD, my strong deliverer, you shield my head in the day of battle. Do not grant the wicked their desires, LORD; do not let their plans succeed. Those who surround me proudly rear their heads; may the mischief of their lips engulf them. May burning coals fall on them; may they be thrown into the fire, into miry pits, never to rise. May slanderers not be established in the land; may disaster hunt down the violent. I know that the LORD secures justice for the poor and upholds the cause of the needy. Surely the righteous will praise your name, and the upright will live in your presence.

Prayers Against Injustice

(Our fight is never against flesh and blood. Therefore, when we pray warfare prayers like this, we must keep in mind that the battle is being waged against demonic spirits that are influencing men on the earth. These type of prayers should be in relationship to all demonic forces working against us unjustly.)

Surely the arm of the LORD is not too short to save, nor his ear too dull to hear. But your iniquities have *separated you from your God; your sins have hidden his face from you, so that he will not hear. For your hands are stained with blood, your fingers with guilt. Your lips have spoken falsely, and your tongue mutters wicked things. No one calls for justice; no one pleads a case with integrity. They rely on empty arguments, they utter lies; they conceive trouble and give birth to evil. They hatch the eggs of vipers and spin a spider's web. Whoever eats their eggs will die, and when one is broken, an adder is hatched. Their cobwebs are useless for clothing; they cannot cover themselves with what they make. Their deeds are evil deeds, and acts of violence are in their hands. Their feet rush into sin; they are swift to shed innocent blood. They pursue evil schemes; acts of violence mark their ways. The way of peace they do not know; there is no justice in their paths. They have turned them into crooked roads; no one who walks along them will know peace. So justice is far from us, and righteousness does not reach us. We look for light, but all is darkness; for brightness, but we walk in deep shadows. Like the blind we grope along the wall, feeling our way like people without eyes. At midday we stumble as if it were twilight; among the strong, we are like the dead. We all growl like bears; we moan mournfully like doves. We look for justice, but find none; for deliverance, but it is far away. For our offenses are many in your sight, and our sins testify against us. Our offenses are ever with us, and we acknowledge our iniquities: rebellion and treachery against the LORD, turning our backs on our God, inciting revolt and oppression, uttering lies our hearts have conceived. So justice is driven back, and righteousness stands at a distance; truth has stumbled in the streets, honesty cannot enter. Truth is nowhere to be found, and whoever shuns evil becomes a prey. The LORD looked and was displeased that there was no justice. He saw that there was no one, he was appalled that there was no one to intervene; so his own arm achieved salvation for him, and his own righteousness sustained him. He put on righteousness as his breastplate, and the helmet of salvation on his head; he put on the garments of vengeance and wrapped himself in zeal as in a cloak. According to what they have done, so will he repay wrath to his enemies and retribution to his foes; he will repay the islands their due. From the west, people will fear the name of the LORD, and from the rising of the sun, they will revere his glory. For he will come like a pent-up flood that the breath of the LORD drives along "The Redeemer will come to Zion, to those in Jacob who repent of their sins," declares the LORD. "As for me, this is my covenant with them," says the LORD. "My Spirit, who is on you, will not depart from you, and my words that I have put in your mouth will always be on your lips, on the lips of your children and on the lips of their descendants—from this time on and forever," says the* LORD. *(Isaiah 59 NIV)*

(Read this entire passage in The Amplified Version of the bible as well.)

Your Confessions and Declaration:

Lord for Your own sake, blot out my sins and remember them no more! (Isaiah 43:25)

In Jehovah I am justified and I will glory. (Isaiah 45:25)

May I have the tongue of the learned to know how to help the weary with a word. May the Lord wake morning by morning and awake my ear to hear as the learned. (Isaiah 50:4)

Lord open my ear and I will not be rebellious nor turn backwards. (Isaiah 50:5)

I am not ashamed for the Lord Jehovah will help Me! I will set my face like a flint, and I will not be ashamed! (Isaiah 50:7)

The Lord Who gives me justice is near. Who will dare to bring charges against me now? Where are my accusers? Let them appear so that they may be brought to justice. (Isaiah 50:8)

Prayers Against Negative Influences

In the Name of Jesus, I come up against and render powerless all negative spirits seeking to work against or manifest within me. I renounce all spirits that have the following characteristics:

Abimelech - spirits that would execute its brothers (he executed 70 of his), family members and peers for the sake of position and prominence. This spirit will stop at nothing even hiring others to assist in its treacherous acts. (Judges 9)

Absalom - all spirits that try to overthrow my position, authority and God-given influence. (2 Samuel 15)

Adam - all spirits attempting to influence me to willfully act against and disobey God's revealed Word to me. (Genesis 3)

Ahab - all spirits that desire to worship false gods and cause me to be passive concerning the true God. (1 Kings 18)

Balaam - all spirits that tempt me to go after filthy lucre and curse and renounce the things of God. (Numbers 22)

Bathsheba - all spirits that would expose my nakedness and cause others to stumble or be tempted in the flesh. (2 Samuel 11)

Belshazzar – those spirits that would cause me to be ignorant and rebellious against God's command and keep me from discerning the handwriting on the wall. (Daniel 5)

Cain - all spirits that are jealous and envious of me coming from my siblings and other peers. Those that wish to murder me with their thoughts, words and even through natural physical manifestations. (Genesis 4)

Delilah - all spirits that use seduction, enticement and betrayal to deceive me. Those that try to take away my strength. (Judges 16)

Demas – spirits that would try to cause me to leave the work of the ministry, the people of God and my assignment in the church, in life or concerning my purpose. (2 Timothy 4)

Eli - spirits that would cause me to become complacent concerning the house of God, the things of God and the purity of God; spiritual familiarity and passivity. That which would cause me to be lax in my health; and indulge in gluttony and over consumption. (1 Samuel 4)

Esau - all spirits that would influence me to disregard, mistreat, and dishonor that which is honorable. Spirits that suppress my level of appreciation for that which is good. Every temptation that will try to get me to sell my birthright and inheritance; those that are assigned to keep me from purpose and walking in my God-given inheritance. (Genesis 25)

Hagar - all spirits that would cause me to be vulnerable and susceptible to being used. Including: slave like situations, over commitments, false burdens and fake friends. (Genesis 16)

Herod & Herodias – spirits that would seek to imprison and execute those who stand for righteousness. All spirits sent to persecute and martyr me and the people of God. (Matthew 14)

Ishmael - all spirits that would cause me to be rejected by my father and siblings. Those that would entice me to be wild and hostile in my conduct and relationships. Those which would influence me to mock others especially those I am intimidated by. (Genesis 16)

Jehoram – Like the spirit of Abimelech this one will execute its brothers, family members and peers for the sake of position and prominence. This man single-handedly executed all six of his brothers. All "cut throat" spirits that would shed the blood of others for selfish motives. (2 Chronicles 21)

Jezebel - all spirits that would try to cause me to do evil, worship false gods, go against the true God and His men and women. Those that want me to kill the prophets of God and give place to false prophets and prophecy. (1 Kings 18)

Joab - spirits that are assigned to conspire against me to cover up truth. Those that wish to murder and secretly annihilate me. Those who work undercover with self-ambition who will do anything to gain a leadership role. (1 Kings 2:5)

Jonah - spirits that cause me to rebel and go against the Word of the Lord and His instruction. (Jonah 1)

Judas – all spirits sent to betray mentors, spiritual parents, teachers and those who have discipled and helped them. This spirit will turn on you especially if rebuked or corrected in front of others. This spirit is also led astray by the love of money. (Matthew 26)

Lot – spirits that would cause me to be greedy and prefer myself over others. Those which will cause me to be attracted to worldly pleasures, susceptible and complacent with sinful situations and environments; those that would trick and deceive me to commit perverse acts against my children and family; spirits of incest. (Genesis 19)

Michal - spirits that will influence me to mock the true worship of God and His people as they worship. Spirits of unfruitfulness and barrenness. (2 Samuel 6)

Miriam and Aaron - spirits that would influence me to be prejudice and speak against the differences of others (unless they are of an immoral and ungodly nature). (Numbers 12)

Nebuchadnezzar - spirits that would cause me to be lifted up in pride and forget where my power comes from. Spirits of insanity. (Daniel 4)

Pharaoh – spirits that try to suppress me; not pay me what I am worth; hold me in bondage; have me work for free or less than that which is fair. (Exodus 8)

Rehoboam - spirits that would keep me from seeking wise council and adhering to it. Those that try to get me to overtax and overburden others. (1 Kings 12)

Samson - spirits that would cause me to disregard my gift and go after fleshly desires. Spirits that deceive, trick and mislead. (Judges 13-15)

Satan – spirits rooted in pride. All spirits of perverseness, wickedness and sin that would try to influence me to exalt myself against God and the knowledge of His Word. (Isaiah 14)

Sennacherib – (He was the King of Assyria and his name means "sin has increased the brothers.") Spirits that come against me and implement siege warfare. All spirits of treacherous acts, exploits and plans against God's people. Those that would try and oppress through dominance. (2 Chronicles 32)

Simon the Sorcerer – spirits that would seek to utilize the gift of God to profit and for selfish reasons and motives. All spirits of prostitution and sell-out demons. (Acts 8)

Prayers for Refuge & Shelter

Lord, I am in trouble! Keep me safe in Your house. Hide me in Your shelter and sacred tent. Then set me high upon a rock. (Psalm 27:5)

How great is the goodness You have stored up for me because I fear You! You lavish it on me as I come to You for protection, blessing me before the watching world. You hide me in the shelter of Your presence, safe from those who conspire against me. You shelter me in Your presence, far from accusing tongues. (Psalm 31:19-20)

Those who come to God Most High for safety will be protected by the Almighty. Lord, You are my place of safety and protection. You are my God and I trust You. You will save me from hidden traps and from deadly diseases. You will cover me with Your feathers, and under Your wings I can hide. Your truth is my shield and protection! (Psalm 91:1-4)

Lord, You are my hiding place! You preserve me from trouble! You surround me with songs of deliverance! (Psalm 32:6-7)

God is my protection and my strength! He always helps me in times of trouble! So, I will not be afraid even if the earth shakes, or the mountains fall into the sea; even if the oceans roar and foam, or the mountains shake at the raging sea! Selah! (Psalm 46:1-3)

But you are a tower of refuge to the poor, O LORD, a tower of refuge to the needy in distress. You are a refuge from the storm and a shelter from the heat. For the oppressive acts of ruthless people are like a storm beating against a wall... (Isaiah 25:4 NLT)

Lord, You are my refuge and my shield! I have put my hope in Your Word. Away from me, you evildoers, for I will keep the commands of my God! Sustain me, my God, according to Your promise, and I will live! Do not let my hopes be dashed. Uphold me, and I will be delivered! I will always have regard for your decrees! (Psalm 119:114-117)

Prayers for Righteous Living

I have faith in Jesus Christ therefore I am the righteousness of God. (Romans 3:22)

May the Lord reward me according to my righteousness: according to the cleanness of my hands has He recompensed me. (2 Samuel 22:21)

Judge me Lord, according to my righteousness, and according to my integrity. (Psalm 7:8)

Lord, You love righteousness, Your countenance beholds the upright. (Psalm 11:7)

Restore my soul Lord and lead me in the paths of righteousness for Your Name's sake. (Psalm 23:3)

I put my trust in You Oh Lord. Never let me be ashamed and deliver me in Your righteousness. (Psalm 31:1)

Lord, I desire to know You and be upright in heart so that Your lovingkindness and righteousness may continue in my life. (Psalm 36:10)

May righteousness be brought forth as the light and my judgment as the noonday. (Psalm 37:6)

Deliver me in my righteousness, and cause me to escape: incline Your ear unto me, and save me. (Psalm 71:2)

I thank You Lord that You execute righteousness and judgment when I am oppressed. (Psalm 103:6)

May wealth, riches, and righteousness endure forever in my house. (Psalm 112:3)

May the gates of righteousness be opened to me so that I may go into them and praise the Lord! (Psalm 118:19)

I long after Your Precepts Lord! May I be quickened with righteousness! (Psalm 119:40)

Lord, Your testimonies are righteous forever; Give me understanding that I may live. (Psalm 119:44)

Lord, my tongue speaks of Your Word for all Your commandments are righteousness. (Psalm 119:172)

Prayers that Get Results

Hear my prayer, Oh Lord, give ear to my supplications: in Your faithfulness and Your righteousness answer me. (Psalm 143:1)

Quicken me, Oh Lord, for Your Name's sake: for Your righteousness' sake bring my soul out of trouble. (Psalm 143:11)

I declare that all the words of my mouth are in righteousness; there is nothing froward or perverse in them. (Proverbs 8:8)

Riches and honor are with me! Yes! Durable riches and righteousness! (Proverbs 8:18)

The righteousness of the perfect will direct his way: but the wicked will fall by his own wickedness. (Proverbs 11:5)

I sow righteousness therefore I have a sure reward. (Proverbs 11:18)

I speak truth therefore I show forth righteousness. (Proverbs 12:17)

May righteousness exalt me and may I not be a reproach because of sin. (Proverbs 14:34)

I follow after righteousness and the Lord loves me. (Proverbs 15:9)

I follow after righteousness and mercy therefore I find life and honor. (Proverbs 21:21)

May righteousness bring me peace, quietness and assurance forever. (Isaiah 32:17)

I do not fear for the Lord is with me! I will not be dismayed for He is God and He will strengthen me. He will help me. He will uphold me with the right Hand of His righteousness. (Isaiah 41:10)

Lord, bring your righteousness near. Do not allow your salvation to tarry. May salvation be in my midst for Your glory! (Isaiah 46:13)

I am established in righteousness. I am far from oppression. I do not fear. Terror will not come near me. (Isaiah 54:14)

May my light break forth as the morning, and my health spring forth speedily! May my righteousness go before me and the glory of the Lord be my reward. (Isaiah 58:8)

In times of mourning, I receive my crown of beauty for ashes, a joyous blessing instead of mourning, joyful praise instead of despair. In my righteousness, I am like a great oak that the LORD has planted for His own glory. (Isaiah 61:3)

I declare that I am wise and I shine as the brightness of the firmament. I turn many to righteousness as the stars for ever and ever. (Daniel 12:3)

I sow in righteousness. I reap mercy and break up the fallow ground. I seek the Lord until He comes and rains down righteousness upon me. (Hosea 10:12)

Let judgment run down as waters, and righteousness as a mighty stream. (Amos 5:24)

May the son of righteousness arise with healing in His wings and release it over my life. (Malachi 4:2)

I am blessed because I thirst and hunger after righteousness and I will be filled. (Matthew 5:6)

I am blessed when I am persecuted for righteousness' sake and the kingdom of heaven belongs to me. (Matthew 5:10)

I seek first the kingdom of God, and His righteousness. Therefore, everything I have need of is added to me. (Matthew 6:33)

I serve the Lord without fear in holiness and righteousness all the days of my life. (Luke 1:74-75)

I awake to righteousness and do not sin. (1 Corinthians 15:34)

I am not unequally yoked with unbelievers. I am righteous. Therefore, I have no fellowship or communion with unrighteousness and darkness. (2 Corinthians 6:14)

I stand clothed with the breastplate of righteousness. (Ephesians 6:14)

I am filled with the fruits of righteousness. (Philippians 1:11)

I flee from covetousness and evil things and follow after righteousness, godliness, faith, love, patience and meekness. (1 Timothy 6:10-11)

I flee youthful lusts. I follow righteousness, faith, charity, peace and all those that call on the Lord with a pure heart. (2 Timothy 2:22)

I receive the inspired Word of God. It is profitable to me for doctrine, for reproof, for correction and for instruction in righteousness. (2 Timothy 3:16)

A crown of righteousness is laid up for me. (2 Timothy 4:8)

I am born of God. Therefore, I do righteousness. (1 John 2:29)

<u>Prayers for God to Be Your Rock</u>

God is my Rock. He is perfect. His ways are judgment. He is a God of truth and without iniquity. Just and right is He. (Deuteronomy 32:4)

I highly esteem God for He is the Rock of my salvation. (Deuteronomy 32:15)

I have not forgotten God. I am mindful that He is my Rock and the God that formed me. (Deuteronomy 32:18)

There is no one that is holy like the Lord and there is no one that is beside Him. Neither is there any Rock like our God. (1 Samuel 2:2)

The God of my rock; in Him will I trust: He is my shield, and the horn of my salvation, my high tower, and my refuge, my Savior; He saves me from violence. (2 Samuel 22:3, Psalm 18:31)

For who is God, but the LORD? And who is a rock, except our God? (2 Samuel 22:32 ESV)

The LORD lives! Praise be to my Rock! Exalted be my God, the Rock, my Savior! (2 Samuel 22:47 NIV)

The LORD is my rock, and my fortress, and my deliverer; my God, my strength, in Him I will trust. He is my buckler, and the horn of my salvation, and my high tower! (Psalm 18:2)

The Lord lives and blessed be my rock; and let the God of my salvation be exalted. (Psalm 18:46)

In God is my salvation and my glory: The Rock of my strength, and my refuge, is in God. (Psalm 62:7)

The LORD is my defense; and my God is the Rock of my refuge. (Psalm 94:22)

Prayers for Strength

Lord, I come to you, for I have been weary and burdened but I know that you will give me rest. I want to know You more and find rest for my soul. (Matthew 11:28-29)

Truly my soul finds rest in God; my salvation comes from Him. (Psalm 62:1 NIV)

"In peace I will lie down and sleep, for you alone, Lord, make me dwell in safety." (Psalm 4:8 NIV)

Lord, I declare that You are the builder of my house so that my labor is not in vain. Watch over my city and may I not toil for food. You love me Lord, so grant me sleep. (Psalm 127:1-2)

I will never get tired of doing that which is good! (2 Thessalonians 3:13)

I will never lack in zeal but I will keep my spiritual fervor and continue to serve the Lord. (Romans 12:11)

Lord, You are my refuge and strength, an ever-present help in trouble! (Psalm 46:1)

I praise You Lord for You have given me rest just as You have promised! Not one of Your words have failed! (1 Kings 8:56)

Prayers that Get Results

Lord, refresh me from being weary and satisfy me so that I will not faint! (Jeremiah 31:25)

Lord, I have been weary, give me strength. I have been weak increase my power. (Isaiah 40:29)

You, God, are awesome in your sanctuary; the God of Israel gives power and strength to His people. Praise be to God! (Psalm 68:35 NIV)

May the Spirit of the Lord help me in my weakness. Holy Spirit help me to pray and intercede for me according to God's will. I love God and I have been called according to His purpose, now work this out for me. (Romans 8:26-28)

I depend on Christ's mighty power that is working within me! (Colossians 1:29)

When my flesh and my heart tries to fail, may God be the strength of my heart and my portion forever! (Psalm 73:26)

I will not become weary in doing good, for at the proper time I will reap a harvest "IF" I do not give up! (Galatians 6:9)

Lord, today I approach Your throne of grace with confidence to receive mercy and to find grace for I am in need. (Hebrews 4:16)

Lord, You are my refuge and my shield! I have put my hope in Your Word! (Psalm 119:114)

In Christ may my heart be refreshed! (Philemon 1:20)

For who is God besides the Lord? And who is the Rock except our God? It is God who arms me with strength and keeps my way secure. (Psalm 18:31-32)

Yes, my soul finds rest in God; my hope comes from Him! (Psalm 62:5)

When I lie down, I will not be afraid! When I lie down, my sleep will be sweet! (Proverbs 3:24)

Lord, may Your Presence go with me and give me rest! (Exodus 33:14)

I will be still and witness "I AM" is God! I exalt God among the nations, I exalt Him in the earth! (Psalm 46:10)

I can do all things through Christ who gives me strength! (Philippians 4:13)

Prayers to Overcome Suffering

Psalm 102
A prayer of an afflicted person who has grown weak and pours out a lament before the LORD.

Hear my prayer, LORD; let my cry for help come to you. Do not hide your face from me when I am in distress. Turn your ear to me; when I call, answer me quickly. For my days vanish like smoke; my bones burn like glowing embers. My heart is blighted and withered like grass; I forget to eat my food. In my distress I groan aloud and am reduced to skin and bones. I am like a desert owl, like an owl among the ruins. I lie awake; I have become like a bird alone on a roof. All day long my enemies taunt me; those who rail against me use my name as a curse. For I eat ashes as my food and mingle my drink with tears because of your great wrath, for you have taken me up and thrown me aside. My days are like the evening shadow; I wither away like grass. But you, LORD, sit enthroned forever; your renown endures through all generations. You will arise and have compassion on Zion, for it is time to show favor to her; the appointed time has come. For her stones are dear to your servants; her very dust moves them to pity. The nations will fear the name of the LORD; all the kings of the earth will revere your glory. For the LORD will rebuild Zion and appear in his glory. He will respond to the prayer of the destitute; he will not despise their plea. Let this be written for a future generation, that a people not yet created may praise the LORD: "The LORD looked down from his sanctuary on high, from heaven he viewed the earth, to hear the groans of the prisoners and release those condemned to death." So the name of the LORD will be declared in Zion and his praise in Jerusalem when the peoples and the kingdoms assemble to worship the LORD. In *the course of my life he broke my strength; he cut short my days. So I said: "Do not take me away, my God, in the midst of my days; your years go on through all generations. In the beginning you laid the foundations of the earth, and the heavens are the work of your hands. They will perish, but you remain; they will all wear out like a garment. Like clothing you will change them and they will be discarded. But you remain the same, and your years will never end. The children of your servants will live in your presence; their descendants will be established before you."*

"For he delivers the needy when they call, the poor and those who have no helper. He has pity on the weak and the needy, and saves the lives of the needy. From oppression to violence he redeems their life; and precious is their blood in his sight." (Psalm 72:12-14)

Prayers for Vindication

(You must consistently keep in perspective who your warfare is against when praying these prayers. As stated already, it is never against flesh and blood. Therefore, as you meditate and even speak aloud these scriptures, think of who your real enemy is. It is Satan and his demonic forces and the battle is in the spirit realm. So pray from the position of that realm using the teachings you have gained from this book.)

Prayers that Get Results

Psalm 109
For the director of music. Of David. A psalm.

My God, whom I praise, do not remain silent, for people who are wicked and deceitful have opened their mouths against me; they have spoken against me with lying tongues. With words of hatred they surround me; they attack me without cause. In return for my friendship they accuse me, but I am a person of prayer. They repay me evil for good, and hatred for my friendship. Appoint someone evil to oppose my enemy; let an accuser stand at their right hand. When they are tried, let them be found guilty, and may their prayers condemn them. May their days be few; may another take their place of leadership. May their children be fatherless and their wife a widow. May their children be wandering beggars; may they be driven from their ruined homes. May a creditor seize all he has; may strangers plunder the fruits of his labor. May no one extend kindness to him or take pity on his fatherless children. May his descendants be cut off, their names blotted out from the next generation. May the iniquity of his fathers be remembered before the LORD; may the sin of his mother never be blotted out. May their sins always remain before the LORD, that he may blot out their name from the earth. For he never thought of doing a kindness, but hounded to death the poor and the needy and the brokenhearted. He loved to pronounce a curse—may it come back on him. He found no pleasure in blessing—may it be far from him. He wore cursing as his garment; it entered into his body like water, into his bones like oil. May it be like a cloak wrapped about him, like a belt tied forever around him. May this be the LORD's payment to my accusers, to those who speak evil of me. But you, Sovereign LORD, help me for your name's sake; out of the goodness of your love, deliver me. For I am poor and needy, and my heart is wounded within me. I fade away like an evening shadow; I am shaken off like a locust. My knees give way from fasting; my body is thin and gaunt. I am an object of scorn to my accusers; when they see me, they shake their heads. Help me, LORD my God; save me according to your unfailing love. Let them know that it is your hand, that you, LORD, have done it. While they curse, may you bless; may those who attack me be put to shame, but may your servant rejoice. May my accusers be clothed with disgrace and wrapped in shame as in a cloak. With my mouth I will greatly extol the LORD; in the great throng of worshipers I will praise him. For he stands at the right hand of the needy, to save their lives from those who would condemn them.

Prayers that Get Results

Psalm 26
Of David.

Vindicate me, LORD, for I have led a blameless life; I have trusted in the LORD and have not faltered. Test me, LORD, and try me, examine my heart and my mind; for I have always been mindful of your unfailing love and have lived in reliance on your faithfulness. I do not sit with the deceitful, nor do I associate with hypocrites. I abhor the assembly of evildoers and refuse to sit with the wicked. I wash my hands in innocence, and go about your altar, LORD, proclaiming aloud your praise and telling of all your wonderful deeds. LORD, I love the house where you live, the place where your glory dwells. Do not take away my soul along with sinners, my life with those who are bloodthirsty, in whose hands are wicked schemes, whose right hands are full of bribes. I lead a blameless life; deliver me and be merciful to me. My feet stand on level ground;

ACKNOWLEDGMENTS

Thank you to Mother Lillian Robinson: You have been the longest standing intercessor of the 5 a.m. P.O.W.! W.O.W.! (Pray on Warrior, Warrior of Wisdom) prayer line. It has been since the year 2000 and counting that I have woken up every single day to hear your voice on the other end of the line. You have stuck with this vision through thick and thin, with few and many, so I say thank you a million times over and here's to you! The world may not know your name but I am sure the spirit realm does!

A special thanks to our other faithful prayer line members: Elder Sheila Carter, Kerry McLaughlin, Terry Phillips, Timothy Phillips, Sadie Fells and Deaconess Emily Robinson. These last two I've named, I am blessed to call my biological mom and my second mom (Emily - my biological aunt). I am blessed to have had such beautiful women of God in my life to raise me. I am glad that during this time of my life, I get to pray with you every single day. Thank you for being a part of my team. You both are blessings from God.

How could I ever forget the people who started me along the path of intercession: Elder Doris Thompson, Prophetess Lurena Jenkins, and Mother

Juanita Clay? As a budding intercessor, you all taught, challenged, provoked and sometimes even "scared" me into embracing this high calling. Mother Clay, you are a mother in Zion and I am glad I am still benefitting from your impartations.

To my late brother-in-law, Reginald Coleman, I hear intercession in some of your music. And to your late wife and my sister-in-law, Charnell Coleman, you could fast and pray with the best of us! The both of you are missed!

To my Madea, the late Ada Fells: You were my mother, my hero and my best friend. You stood in the gap for me when I didn't know how to stand for myself.

Thanks to my previous pastor, Tom Bynum: You prophesied that I was an intercessor before I even knew what the word meant. I'll never forget how God has used you and Apostle Samantha to impart much in my life.

Thanks to my husband, John Coleman. Your love for God keeps me wanting more of Him too. You have taught me what it means to truly be faithful. A faithful man, who can find? I found him!

To my wonderful children: Christian Kilan, Kennedy Jordan, Ca'Koia Blessing Alexandria, Rain Blessings Alexandria and Jream Alexander, thanks

ACKNOWLEDGMENTS

for putting up with the loud 5 am noises that are often in our house because mom has gotten so pumped up during her time of intercession that she has forgotten others live in the same house. Although, the expressions on your faces were not the most pleasant, thanks for never complaining! You are the best!

To: Bishop I.V. and Pastor Bridget Hilliard, your teachings on the principles of faith and your tenacity to emphasize integrity and excellence has taught me to persevere, and inspired the confidence in me to always win as I walk by faith!

To: Apostle John Eckhardt for allowing me to be a part of your Periscope *50 States, 50 Days Prayer Initiative*. Thank you for who you are and all of what you bring to the body of Christ!

To the dedicated people that have stood with us and shared their wisdom: Drs. Meredith & Marilyn Shackelford, you helped us through a tragic time in our lives and we will never forget that! Pastors Eric & Winifred Ashby, you have been long time friends as well as spiritual advisors, thank you!

Thanks to my entire Kingdom Church International family; every elder, minister and member. I love you dearly and you are the best church family that a pastor can have! My prayer for you always is Hebrews 6:10.

Thank you to every partner to our ministry and all the Doers who follow me on social media. It is because of your faithful support of our vision that John and I are able to do what God has called us to do. God will not forget your ministry to us!

I know that I am the intercessor I have become today because of the countless people that have deposited spiritual truths and imparted the insight needed to persevere and be effective in this anointing. To you I say thank you!

ADDITIONAL PRAYER RESOURCES

1. *30 Day Praying for Your Children Challenge*, By Bob Hostetler
   www.reviveourhearts.com

2. *Seven Things to Pray for Your Children*,
   www.desiringGod.org

3. *31 Specific Prayers for Children*,
   www.Christianpost.com

4. *Raising a Standard Against Untimely Death*,
   www.prayercamp.blogspot.com website

5. *Prayers Against Untimely Deaths*,
   http://christ-online.blogspot.com/2007/12/prayers-against-untimely-death.html

AUTHOR BIOGRAPHICAL INFORMATION

Dr. Kisia L. Coleman says, "I love ministry! I love what ministry does to and for people. The services, the messages, the worship, the fellowship, and most of all, THE IMPACT! And I just want to play a part in making that impact happen!"

In 2003, Dr. Kisia received her Masters in Ministry from Midwest Christian College & Seminary. She later became a teacher in the college, where her focus was in Leadership Training. In 2011 she was conferred an Honorary Doctor of Divinity from the Institute for Christian Works Bible College and Seminary, an accredited institution, by the World Council of Postsecondary and Religious Education. She is a licensed and ordained minister of the gospel and is recognized under the authority of New Light Christian Center Church & the Association of Independent Ministries (A.I.M.) of Houston, Texas.

Dr. Kisia has served executives and CEOs as a Personal Assistant in various fields, including the healthcare, legal, financial, and religious arenas; including two mega-churches. She has found that her greatest joy is serving in ministry. In January of 2006, working alongside her husband, Dr. John, she helped to pioneer Kingdom Church International, affectionately known as KCI by its members. As founders of this non-denominational, multicultural community of believers, their mission is to: "Empower God's people for Kingdom living and for

Kingdom advancement in the earth." In May 2014 they acquired their own building in the inner city of Chicago making their presence evident in both the city and the suburbs.

Additionally, Dr. Kisia's responsibilities include: Executive Administrator, Special Events Director, and the founder of *M.O.D.E.L.* (Mentoring Our Daughters & Equipping Ladies*)*, a ministry for women; *The Princess Paradigm*, a mentoring ministry for girls; and *L.E.A.D* (Leaders Empowered to Accelerate & Dominate), a leadership training class for Kingdom leaders. In February of 2000, Dr. Kisia began a Phone Conference Prayer Ministry *(P.O.W. W.OW.* – Pray on Warrior, Warrior of Wisdom), which is a one-hour, daily intercessory phone conference. Their motto is, "Every day we pray!" Since its inception, intercessors have been gathering together every day at 5 a.m. weekdays and 7 a.m. weekends to bombard the heavens with intercession.

Dr. Kisia has spearheaded many initiatives including *Waiting to Excel Back to School Backpack & Supply* Giveaway and *Bringing Joy to the Community* outreach programs. Her efforts with global partners has provided for opportunities to bring aid to people in the Philippines, Haiti, Bulgaria, South Africa, Croatia, Peru and Uganda, raising tens of thousands of dollars to help families in need. She is an entrepreneur and the founder of *KishKnows, Inc. - The Bright Idea Company* which has several divisions including print publishing, online consumer products, empowerment resources and coaching services. She is the author of *The DO IT Mandate - Defeating the Delays to Destiny* book and accompanying workbook; as well as *The Do It Book Writing & Publishing Series* with online courses and most recently *Prayers That Get Results – The DOERS Guide to Turning Tragedy into Triumph and Overcoming the Failures in Life! Volume 1* book. These inspiring resources of empowerment provide encouragement as well as the necessary tools for all of those that want to realize success in life and be doers of the Word and not just hearers only.

Some of her other accomplishments include: Certified Life & Leadership Coach, Creator and Developer of *The Do It Master Motivational & Task Mobile App* for the iPhone and Google platforms; and the graduate of *Kingdom University* (Dr. Cindy Trimm). In both October 2012 and October 2013 she was the proud recipient of the *Literary Award* given by the Association of Independent Ministries (A.I.M.) in Houston, Texas.

Dr. Kisia is an innovative visionary and a straight-talking communicator. She is proving her paradigm of being a Christ-like model to others through serving and doing is what greatness and success are really all about. She and her husband live in a suburb of Chicago and are the parents of five children: two boys and three girls; which include two orphaned nieces and a nephew.

AUTHOR CONTACT INFORMATION

For more information, or to see a list of our products and services please contact:

Business

LinkedIn: Kisia L. Coleman
KishKnows, Inc.
www.kishknows.com
708-252-DOIT

Personal

Kisia Fells Coleman
www.facebook.com/kishknows
www.twitter.com/kishknows
Periscope @kishknows

Ministry

Kingdom Church International
P.O. Box 596
Park Forest, Illinois 60466
708-872-8KCI
www.trykci.org
info@trykci.org

www.ingramcontent.com/pod-product-compliance
Lightning Source LLC
LaVergne TN
LVHW041624070426
835507LV00008B/438